ART, MYTH, AND CULTURE:
GREEK VASES FROM SOUTHERN COLLECTIONS

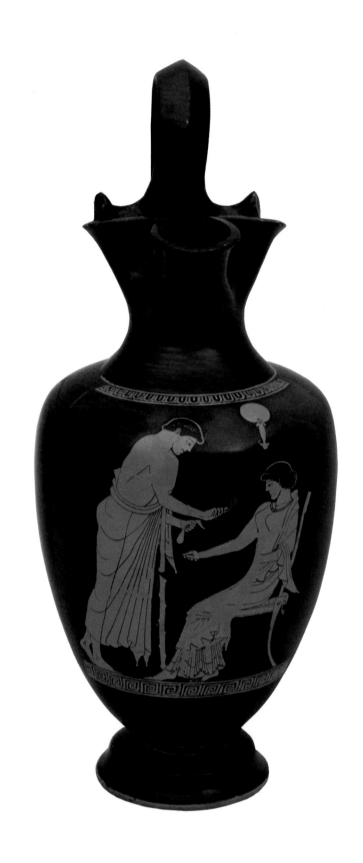

63. Attic Red-Figure Oinochoe

ART, MYTH, AND CULTURE
GREEK VASES FROM SOUTHERN COLLECTIONS

INTRODUCTION AND CATALOGUE BY H. A. SHAPIRO

NEW ORLEANS MUSEUM OF ART
TULANE UNIVERSITY

1981

2000 copies of the catalog were printed for the exhibition
Art, Myth, and Culture: Greek Vases from Southern Collections
This publication was made possible, in part, by a grant from the National
Endowment for the Humanities, Washington, D.C., a Federal Agency,
and a generous donation from Mr. and Mrs. Arthur Q. Davis, New Orleans.

Designed by Jerry Schuppert, Printing Production Service, Inc., New Orleans
Drawings by Susan Levy
Typography by Green's Typographic Service, New Orleans
Printed in the United States of America by Franklin Printing Co., Inc., New Orleans
Binding by Walter W. Eckert Binder, New Orleans

LIBRARY OF CONGRESS CATALOGING IN PUBLICATION DATA

Shapiro, H. A. (Harvey Alan), 1949-

Art, myth, and culture.

  Bibliography: p.
  1. Vases, Greek — Exhibitions.
2. Vase-painting, Greek — Exhibitions.
3. Mythology, Greek, in art — Exhibitions.
4. Vases — Southern States — Exhibitions.
I. New Orleans Museum of Art.   II. Tulane University.
III. Title.
NK4621.N48N487   738.3'82'0938074016335   81-82732
ISBN 0-89494-012-0   AACR2

front cover: Detail No. 30 Attic Red-Figure Bell-Krater
title page: Detail No. 13 Attic Black-Figure Eye-Cup

Preface and Acknowledgements

Ever since Keats wrote his celebrated "Ode on a Grecian Urn" over a century and a half ago, the beauty and perfection of Greek vases have exercised a fascination for the aesthete, the connoisseur, and even the casual viewer. In so many ways a fine Greek vase seems to capture in miniature the highest ideals of the Classical civilization that produced it: the shape embodying rhythm, harmony, balance, and proportion; the draughtsmanship a model of refinement, wit, delicacy, and precision. There is another quality, less apparent, which is also quintessentially Greek: these vases, that we regard as art objects and place on display in museums, were made to be used, and in every instance the shape was carefully designed to follow function and to be as practical as it is beautiful.

Greek vases are representatives of their culture in other ways often less easy for the contemporary viewer to apprehend. As Keats asked of his urn, "What leaf-fringed legend haunts about thy shape?" so we may wonder at the endlessly varied array of scenes which comprise the Greek vase-painter's repertoire. It is this aspect of Greek vases that the present exhibition seeks to explore: the vivid glimpses of the everyday life of the Greeks afforded by some, and, on others, the tradition of heroic myths and legends which permeated Greek culture and became a rich legacy to later Western literature and art.

This exhibition is the fruit of a cooperative effort sponsored by the New Orleans Museum of Art and Tulane University, made possible by the generous support of the National Endowment for the Humanities, Washington, D.C. A generous donation from Mr. and Mrs. Arthur Q. Davis, lenders to the exhibition, assisted in the publication of this catalogue.

In keeping with the guidelines of the National Endowment for the Humanities, the catalogue is intended primarily for the general reader, rather than the scholar of Greek vases, though we trust that the latter will also find much of interest here. For this reason, certain information which would occupy a large portion of a more scholarly work — detailed discussions of the objects' state of preservation, technique, ornament, and stylistic attribution — has been kept to a minimum or, in many cases, omitted. Since, however, more than half the vases are here illustrated and discussed for the first time, we hope their appearance in this catalogue will encourage other scholars to undertake the full publications they deserve.

The New Orleans Museum of Art is grateful to the many individuals whose assistance and cooperation made this exhibition possible. As guest curator, Professor Alan Shapiro, formerly of Tulane University, now on the Humanities faculty of the Stevens Institute of Technology, conceived the idea for the exhibition, selected the objects, and was the principal author of the catalogue. Professor Shapiro was assisted in locating the vases and preparing the catalogue by several scholars to whom thanks are recorded here: Dr. Dietrich von Bothmer and Andrew Clark of the Metropolitan Museum of Art; Dr. Margaret Ellen Mayo of the Virginia Museum of Fine Arts; Professor D. A. Amyx of the University of California, Berkeley; Professor Robert F. Sutton of Loyola University of Chicago; and Professor Robert A. Koch of Princeton University. We are especially grateful to three scholars who lent their expertise by contributing entries to the catalogue: Professor Karl Kilinski II of Southern Methodist University; Dr. Jenifer Neils of the Cleveland Museum of Art; and Professor Lucy Turnbull of the University of Mississippi. The handsome design of the catalogue is the work of Jerry Schuppert of Printing Production Service, Inc., New Orleans.

We are greatly indebted to Edward Diefenthal for the superb photographs of his own and several other vases which appear in this publication. As Project Researcher, Susan E. Levy has contributed in innumerable ways to the success of the project, not least with her skillful drawings for the catalogue. From the inception the cooperation of Tulane University, particularly Dr. S. Frederick Starr, Vice President for Academic Affairs, and Professor Joe Park Poe, Chairman, Department of Classical Languages, has been gratifying, and the collaboration between the museum and university most rewarding. A special thanks to William A. Fagaly, Assistant Director of Art, New Orleans Museum of Art, for his considerable efforts both in the organization of the exhibition and the preparation of the catalogue.

Finally, we are most grateful to the sixteen institutions and seven private collectors without whose readiness to lend these fragile objects and entrust them to our care this exhibition would not have been possible.

E. JOHN BULLARD
Director
New Orleans Museum of Art

Contents

Frontispiece   2

Preface & Acknowledgements   5

Lenders to the Exhibition   8

Introduction   9

Catalogue of the Exhibition   11

    Gods and Goddesses   13

    Dionysos and his Circle   35

    Herakles   57

    Heroes   77

    Cults and Festivals   101

    War and Combat   117

    Everyday Life   127

    Sports   141

    Revelry, Love and Marriage   157

Glossary of Shapes in the Exhibition   171

Lenders to the Exhibition

The Ackland Art Museum, University of North Carolina at Chapel Hill
Birmingham Museum of Art
Cummer Gallery of Art
Dallas Museum of Fine Arts
Duke University Museum of Art
Archer M. Huntington Art Gallery, University of Texas at Austin
The Lowe Art Museum
The Museum of Fine Arts, Houston
New Orleans Museum of Art
North Carolina Museum of Art
John and Mable Ringling Museum of Art
San Antonio Museum Association
Tulane University
The University Museums, University of Mississippi
University of Arkansas Museum
Virginia Museum of Fine Arts

Mr. and Mrs. Arthur Q. Davis
Gilbert M. Denman, Jr.
Mr. and Mrs. Edward L. Diefenthal
Costas Lemonopoulos
Mrs. Nathan Polmer
Dr. Norbert Schimmel
Private Collection

Introduction

Painted pottery constitutes our most extensive body of remains of the material culture of Ancient Greece. Even when a vase has been smashed to pieces, the fabric of the baked clay is essentially indestructible, and it may often be pieced back together. Fire, the chief agent of destruction in antiquity of more perishable objects, only strengthens a vase which has once been fired in the kiln. In periods and in regions when life in Greece was at a subsistence level, precluding the manufacture of artifacts in bronze and other expensive materials, clay was always plentiful, and clay vessels, because of their utilitarian value, continued always to be made. Since the clay in many parts of Greece is particularly fine, and pottery is easily transported and useful for transporting other goods (oil, wine, grain), Greek vases travelled to every part of the Mediterranean, and excavations of the last hundred years have uncovered many more vases outside of Greece than within it.

The manufacture of pottery in Greece was virtually uninterrupted from the later Neolithic period (fourth millenium B.C.) to the end of antiquity. Within that broad spectrum of time, the vases in this exhibition represent a relatively narrow span of about 200 years, from ca. 600 to 400 B.C., when Greek civilization was at its height and produced a body of literature, art, and philosophic and scientific thought that would have a lasting impact on later Western culture. To understand the place of these vases within the scope of Greek painted pottery, a brief sketch of its historical development may be useful.

The beginning of the historical period in Greece is traditionally put in the second half of the eighth century B.C. This period followed several centuries of "Dark Ages," the aftermath of the collapse of Mycenaean civilization about 1200-1100 B.C., and was marked by the reintroduction of writing, in an early form of the Greek alphabet which is familiar to us, the establishment of trading contacts and Greek colonies in South Italy, Sicily, the Near East, and the region around the Black Sea, and a general upswing in population and material prosperity. This is probably also the period to which the earliest Greek literature, the Homeric *Iliad* and *Odyssey*, belongs. This half century, 750-700 B.C., coincides with the ceramic phase known as Late Geometric. Pots, many of them enormous kraters and amphoras which were used as grave markers, are decorated mostly with bands of neatly drawn geometric patterns - triangles, meanders (the "Greek key"), lozenges, etc. This is the culmination of a style that had begun several centuries earlier and now for the first time also includes small figured scenes, mainly funerary in content. There were schools of Geometric pottery all over Greece, but the largest and most sophisticated was in Attica. It seems possible that because Athens, alone of all Mycenaean citadels, was not utterly destroyed at the end of the Bronze Age, there was not the same discontinuity of civilization as elsewhere in Greece; Athens' Dark Ages were less dark than in other areas, and the city emerged into the light of history already as a leading artistic center.

But Athens' ceramic preeminence was short-lived, for by 700 potters and painters in Corinth were starting to draw inspiration from the older art of the Near East, just now becoming accessible, and to create a fabric that would, in the course of the seventh century, gain enormous popularity around the Mediterranean. Corinthian potters had a virtual monopoly on the newly opened trade routes. Athens was not unaffected by this so-called Orientalizing style, and although Proto-Attic pottery, as this phase is known, was not a commercial succeess, it was crucially important in another way. It produced some of the earliest experiments in mythological narrative, that is, the translation of epic poetry, some of it written down but most circulating in an oral tradition, into the visual arts. Other Orientalizing fabrics, including Proto-Corinthian, shared in the experiment, though none with the inventiveness of Proto-Attic, and by the time the century was out, the framework of a whole mythological repertoire had been laid. The occasional inclusion of inscriptions naming the figures reflects a sense of urgency on the part of the painters that their narrative scenes be recognized and correctly understood.

In the competition for foreign markets, the pendulum began to swing back to Athens about 600. The black-figure technique - painting the figures in a shiny black glaze against the light ground of the clay, details incised with a sharp tool - though first developed in Corinth, was perfected by Athenian painters in the late seventh century and early sixth. This, together with a variety of new shapes (some adapted from Corinthian ones), made Attic pottery suddenly very desirable. Some Corinthian potters and painters, seeing the handwriting on the wall, probably moved to Athens, giving added momentum to the Athenian ceramic industry. Solon's legislation offering a hospitable welcome to foreign artists and craftsmen who emigrated to Athens insured a supply of young talent. The final result was that by 550, Corinthian export of pottery had ceased, and for the next hundred and fifty years no city in Greece besides Athens made pottery for other than local use in any significant quantity.

The production of Attic black-figure, which had its heyday in the third quarter of the sixth century, probably enjoyed the support of the enlightened Athenian tyrant Peisistratos and his sons. The art of stone sculpture also flourished in Athens at this time, and much building activity, both secular and religious, took place as well. If Athens did not produce any of the major poets of Archaic Greece, it was nevertheless an enthusiastic audience for the works of older and contemporary foreign poets, some of whom were entertained at the Tyrants' courts. In Athens under Peisistratos authoritative editions of Homer may have been made for the first time, and recitations of Homeric poetry were part of the Panathenaic festival. This literary interest is evident in the hundreds of myth scenes on black-figure vases, drawn from the Trojan Cycle, other epic sagas, and especially the life and deeds of Herakles.

Even as black-figure was at its height, about 530, a new technique was invented - red-figure: the background now covered with black glaze, the figures reserved in the orange color of the clay, and the detail painted with glaze rather than incised. The inventors had of course all grown up on black-figure, and for twenty years or so many of the best artists practiced both techniques. For a half century, ca. 530-480, the two were made side by side, black-figure in huge quantities, though of steadily declining quality, red-figure gaining both in quantity *and* quality, with phases of ever greater originality and technical perfection following in rapid succession. This enormous output was sustained primarily thanks to the insatiable demand and seemingly limitless resources of buyers in Etruria. The Etruscans at this time were enjoying the zenith of their prosperity and power in north Italy, and, beside their keen appreciation for Greek art, were apparently enthusiastic students of Greek mythology who particularly wanted elaborate myth scenes on their vases. Most of the vases they bought they took to their graves, and thousands have been unearthed by archaeologists and tomb-robbers over the past 150 years.

The first half century of red-figure was characterized not only by stylistic experimentation, as both painting and sculpture strove to break free from the confines of Archaic art, but by a great proliferation in the variety of non-mythological subject matter. Genre scenes such as athletes taking exercise, boys at school, symposia, and love-making give us a more intimate look at the daily lives of the Greeks than had any source, written or visual, ever before.

At the same time that Athens was entering its age of greatest achievement, with victories over the Persian Empire in 490 and again in 480/79, the Etruscans were just going into eclipse. They were expelled from Rome in 509 and lost a major naval battle in 474. During Athens' Early Classical period, 480-450, demand for exports of red-figure vases may have slowed, though by no means ceased. A

second possible explanation for the gradual falling off in the quality of Attic vase-painting after 480 may be offered by the concomitant rise of monumental wall-painting as a major art. Such paintings, done in a fresco technique not unlike that of the Italian Renaissance, decorated shrines and other public buildings, bringing their masters much greater celebrity than was possible for a vase-painter. Thus it is reasonable to assume that a young painter of exceptional promise would try to make his fortune as a wall-painter rather than in a potter's shop. Unfortunately not a scrap of these large scale paintings in Athens has survived, though recent spectacular finds in Macedonia give some hint of what was possible in this medium.

The last few red-figure painters who could be said to approach in stature those of the Late Archaic were working about 460-440 B.C. It is ironic that by the period of the Parthenon (448-432), when Greek sculpture is traditionally held to have reached its acme, the vase-painter's art was long past its prime and had nearly exhausted itself. The massive upheaval of the Peloponnesian War (431-404) put an end to most of the overseas markets for Attic pottery; some painters and potters moved to the Greek cities of South Italy; and potters' shops in Athens catered to a beleaguered city which put on a good face by erecting splendid monuments on the Acropolis, but probably had little use for extravagance in private art. Only the workshops specializing in white funerary lekythoi, grim signs of the times, seem to have prospered.

Yet the subject matter of later Attic red-figure is not at all impoverished, and in fact adds new dimensions to the old repertoire. The domestic life of women is now documented more fully than before, as more vases appear to have been made for female customers. The great tragedies of Sophocles and Euripides were produced during these years, and their influence may sometimes be detected on vases. A new interest in personified abstractions (Justice, Persuasion, Good Repute, etc.), probably emanating from the schools of philosophy and rhetoric, leads to some of the first forays into the complex realm of allegorical art. The intellectual climate in Athens in the later fifth century was surely more stimulating than at almost any other time in history, and even if the vase-painters were not among the great creative minds, one would like to think that at least a little of the excitement rubbed off on them.

Catalogue of the Exhibition

All dimensions are in centimeters. The maximum diameter is given unless otherwise specified. Bracketed numbers in the text refer to catalogue numbers. All catalogue entries are written by H. A. Shapiro unless signed otherwise. The following abbreviations have been used:

Beazley, *ABV*:   J. D. Beazley, *Attic Black-figure Vase-painters* (Oxford 1956)

Beazley, *ARV²*:   J. D. Beazley, *Attic Red-figure Vase-painters*, 2nd Edition (Oxford 1963)

Beazley, *Paralipomena*:   J. D. Beazley, *Paralipomena* (Oxford 1971)

Brommer, *Vasenlisten*[3]:   Frank Brommer, *Vasenlisten zur griechischen Heldensage*, 3rd Edition (Marburg 1973)

CVA: *Corpus Vasorum Antiquorum*

Gods and Goddesses

The Greeks were one of the few ancient peoples who conceived their gods anthropomorphically and often represented them in art, both by themselves and interacting with mortal men. Not only did the Greek gods *look* more like humans than most, they also behaved very much like ordinary men and women and were subject to the same shortcomings and foibles: envy, lust, greed, anger, vindictiveness.

The origin and genealogy of all the gods, as well as the character traits and spheres of interest of each, were set out by Homer, Hesiod in his *Theogony*, and in a series of Early Archaic poems addressed to the various divinities, called the Homeric *Hymns*. Greek artists drew their initial inspiration from these sources, though the image of a god or goddess might change considerably over time, along with changing styles and conceptions in art. Thus, for example, Aphrodite was shown nude only beginning in the mid-fourth century, having been up to that time just as modest and proper as any other goddess.

All the gods appear in vase-painting, some much more often than others, and most in particular contexts. Their relative popularity does not necessarily correspond to their seniority, status, or mythological importance. By far the most often represented divinity is Dionysos, who is of little or no consequence in Homer and Hesiod (see p. 35). Very seldom do all or most of the Olympian gods appear together, though Homer pictures the assembled gathering many times. One myth which does bring them together on some vases is the Gigantomachy (see [3]), and they are occasionally seen as a group welcoming the newly deified Herakles to Olympos (see [26]).

Zeus appears in several different scenes, most notably giving birth to Athena from his head, though this subject is popular more because of Athena than because of Zeus. Curiously, one of Zeus' primary activities on red-figure vases is a somewhat undignified amorous pursuit of mortal women [1]. His brothers, Hades and Poseidon, are not very often seen, though the latter is also an ardent womanizer.

Zeus' wife Hera appears often in only one scene, the Judgment of Paris [37].

Of the younger generation of Olympians, Athena is far more often represented than any other, for two reasons. As the city goddess of Athens, she is an essential figure in many aspects of Athenian cult and art. She strides vigorously across every Panathenaic amphora (see [40] and p. 101). Excerpts from the Gigantomachy often focus on her [3], and in many of the myths dealing with Attic mythology she plays a role [4]. In addition, Athena is the patroness of heroes, not just of Attic heroes like Theseus, but of all heroes, and especially Herakles [24, 26]. In Homer she lends encouragement to Odysseus, Telemachos, Achilles, and Diomedes, and on vases she appears with Perseus [38], Jason, and others. Together with Aphrodite and Hera she appears at the Judgment of Paris [37], one of the rare myths that puts her in a not altogether favorable light.

Hermes is very often seen on vases [5, 23, 27, 37, 38], because of his roles as messenger, companion of heroes, and conveyor of the souls of the dead, but he is always an adjunct, rather than the center of attention. The twins Artemis and Apollo are often shown together [2]; when not playing his lyre, Apollo can often be found chasing women, like his father and uncle. Ares, as expected, appears only in scenes of combat, and then not often, except trying in vain to help his son Kyknos [24].

Two of the most often represented divinities in Attic red-figure are personified abstractions: Nike (Victory) and Eros (Love). In black-figure, the winged Nike had appeared as a companion, almost an attribute, of Zeus. She can allude not only to victory in battle, but in athletic contests as well, and she is often seen with a young athlete. But most often she is shown by herself [8, 9], carrying torches, a musical instrument, or other attribute. Eros makes a sudden appearance in red-figure just after 500 and then is ubiquitous, either singly or in groups or Erotes. He accompanies his mother Aphrodite and is often a part of women's scenes [6], though he is also shown pursuing boys and, like Nike and Apollo, is a devoté of the lyre.

1

Attic Red-Figure Amphora of Panathenaic Shape

Collection of the Birmingham Museum of Art, Gift of Mrs. Herbert Rydings, Jr.
and Hirschl and Adler Gallery, New York (57.263)
Attributed to the Tyszkiewicz Painter [Bothmer]
500-490 B.C.
Height: 39.3 cm.
Diameter: 26.3 cm.

Side A: Zeus pursuing a woman
Side B: Man and woman at an altar

On side A, Zeus strides forward, bent over slightly as if swooping down on the woman, who raises her right hand in a gesture of fear and aversion and runs off to the right. The god is identified by the scepter, the symbol of kingly power, and by the wreath of what seem stylized oak leaves on his head. He holds the scepter near its lower end, as if to reach out and bar the woman's way. The identity of the woman is uncertain without an inscription or any distinguishing attributes. Zeus' loves were legendary, in every sense of the word; the younger Olympian gods were his children by various goddesses and nymphs, and his human mistresses were innumerable. Every noble family in the Greek world traced its ancestry back to a hero born of a god and a mortal woman, and more of them claimed Zeus as ancestor than any other god. In a comic interlude in the *Iliad*, Zeus' wife Hera seduces him on a mountaintop in order to distract his attention from the battlefield of Troy. He expresses his sudden lust for her rather tactlessly, giving a list of goddesses and mortal woman he has loved, "But never with as great a passion as I now feel for you!"

The scene on the reverse is a complete contrast. A man and a woman stand on either side of an altar on which a fire is burning. He leans on his walking stick and holds out a phiale, a cup for pouring libations to the gods, which she fills with wine from a jug. The figures are at ease, the atmosphere calm; they may be man and wife sacrificing on some family occasion (birth of a child?) or at a family celebration during one of the great Athenian festivals. The contrast between the two scenes is surely intentional: on one side the two mortals, harmoniously and soberly carrying out a traditional rite, an embodiment of the normal pattern of human relationships with one another and with the gods; on the other side, the violent expression of an unequal passion. Zeus' heavily muscled legs, broad shoulders and thick neck embody the irresistable power of the god, but also the equally irresistable power of love, violent in its onslaught and its expression. Against this double force she is helpless; she runs, but there is no escape. In other versions of this scene Zeus carries a thunderbolt, the annihilating weapon of supreme power, a reminder that for mortals (creatures of a day, *ephemerai*, the gods call them) even the love of gods is a dangerous as their anger. The painter may have been influenced by early tragic drama, in which the difference in power between gods and mortals is a mainspring of the action. In *Prometheus Bound*, produced slightly later than this vase, Aeschylus shows the sufferings of Io, a girl whom Zeus loved and Hera transformed into a cow and drove wandering over the earth in perpetual torment. The horrified chorus of sea nymphs prays, "May I never share the bed of Zeus or attract a god as lover. Only in an equal match is there no fear."

LUCY TURNBULL

Bibliography: Beazley, *ARV²* 292, 35. For gods as lovers of mortal women: S. Kaempf-Dimitriadou, *Die Liebe der Götter in der attischen Kunst des V. Jahrhunderts v. Chr.* (Bern 1979).

detail

Side A

Side B

2

Attic Black-Figure Neck-Amphora

Collection of Costas Lemonopoulos, St. Petersburg, courtesy of the
  Museum of Fine Arts of St. Petersburg
Unattributed
Ca. 515-505 B.C.
    Height: 39.4 cm.

Side A: Apollo kitharoidos and four goddesses
Side B: Scythian archer between horsemen

Apollo is the patron of the arts, and especially of music. He is closely associated with the nine Muses, whom he often leads in a dance at a gathering of the gods or a celebration for a hero. His favorite instrument is the kithara, or lyre, and whenever the god is shown making music, it is always on the lyre. Other figures are sometimes depicted with a lyre on Attic vases, such as Nike [9], or the boy Tithonos, who was ravished by the goddess of the dawn, but a stately male lyre-player in a long garment is generally Apollo. Though sometimes portrayed as a nude athletic type, especially in sculpture of the fifth century, Apollo is always draped when he plays the lyre. **On side A** of the Lemonopoulos amphora he wears a *chiton* and, over it, a *himation* decorated with large red dots. He also has a red fillet in his hair, and a cord attached to the instrument hangs from his right hand. The god is surrounded by two pairs of female figures, all dressed alike in a long *chiton*, also decorated with red dots. Two hold an object which looks like *krotala*, or metal castanets. A graceful doe stands beside each pair of women. It is difficult to say who these might be. The presence both of Apollo and of the does makes one think of Artemis, the god's sister and goddess of the hunt, but presumably she would somehow be singled out from the others. Four of the Muses, perhaps, drawn by an artist concerned more with symmetry than completeness?

In contrast to this peaceful and musical scene, **side B** features three warriors preparing to depart. The standing figure in the center carries bow and quiver and wears a short *chiton* and a pointed leather cap with long ear flaps. The hat and his pointy beard mark him as a Scythian archer, a native of South Russia probably employed at Athens as a mercenary. In the fifth century, Scythians appear to have served as policemen in Athens, but their frequent earlier appearances on black-figure vases of the later sixth century may reflect a policy of the tyrant Peisistratos in hiring foreign mercenaries from the North. Before the time of the Persian Wars, the Athenians had had little experience of archery (see [59]), while the Scythians' skill with the bow was proverbial. The other two warriors flanking the archer, both mounted, wear Corinthian helmets and appear to be standard Greek soldiers.

The vase belongs to the period of the Leagros Group, a large body of mostly neck-amphoras and hydrias, produced by one or several closely related black-figure workshops contemporary with the red-figure "Pioneers."

Bibliography: *Ancient Art* (Sale Catalogue, Sotheby Park Bernet, New York, 1980) lot 173, ill. On Scythian archers: M. F. Vos, *Scythian Archers in Archaic Attic Vase-Painting* (Groningen 1963).

Side A

Side B

17

3

Attic Black-Figure Plate

Collection of The Museum of Fine Arts, Houston, the Annette Finnigan
   Collection (37-19)
Assigned to the Segment Class [H. Hoffmann]
Ca. 520-510 B.C.
   Diameter: 23.5 cm.

Athena battling the giant Enkelados

The scene is an excerpt from the Battle of Gods and Giants, one of the most popular mythological scenes in Archaic Greek art. The Giants, children of Ge, Mother Earth, tried to storm Mount Olympos, but were repulsed by the combined effort of all the Olympian gods and goddesses, with the help of Herakles. By convention certain gods battle certain giants, and when Athena's opponent is named by inscription, he is Enkelados. Otherwise Enkelados has no distinguishing traits or attributes.

Athena wears a belted *chiton*, *himation*, and a high-crested Attic helmet. Her aegis is draped over her extended left arm, serving as a shield, and in her right hand, obscured by the drapery, she wields a spear. Enkelados, who has fallen to one knee, tries to protect himself with a shield whose device is a satyr's head. He wears a corselet over a short *chiton*, which has short sleeves and a patterned skirt. His helmet is of the Corinthian type, which is meant to be pulled down over nose and cheeks, but has been knocked askew and almost off by the force of Athena's blow. The Giant too holds a spear but is powerless to use it. In Archaic art, the Giants are not represented as monstrous, or even of great stature, but instead look no different from heavily armed Greek hoplites. Only in later art, as on the Pergamon Altar, do they sometimes take on a grotesque appearance, as the poet Hesiod imagined them.

Attic plates were not functional, but were rather plaques, made for dedicatory purposes. The Houston example has two suspension holes near the top, which suggests that it was perhaps intended to be hung up in a sanctuary. Quite possibly it was dedicated to the city goddess, Athena, on the Acropolis. Certainly the subject is appropriate for such a purpose and is one which occurs on a number of vases and fragments excavated on the Acropolis. The Gigantomachy, including the Athena-Enkelados group, was the subject of several large-scale architectural sculptures in the sixth and fifth centuries. One of the most notable of these is a marble pediment which decorated the Old Temple of Athena on the north side of the Acropolis, also called Doerpfeld's Temple or the Peisistratid Temple, because it was probably built in the time of Hippias and Hipparchos, sons of the Tyrant Peisistratos (ca. 527-510). The splendid striding Athena from that composition is well preserved, and her pose and dress are similar to those of the Athena on this plate. The traditional date for this pediment, about 520, has recently been questioned by some scholars who would push it toward the end of the Peisistratid tyranny, about 510, or even later, regarding it as a product of the young Athenian democracy after 510. If the earlier date is correct, however, it would be reasonable to ask whether the Houston plate could have been inspired by the central group of the pediment and have hung not far from it in Athena's sanctuary on the Acropolis.

The decoration of this plate is akin to that of the Segment Class, a group of stemless cups in which the picture fills the whole interior and there is often an exergue below the principal scene. Here two leaping dolphins occupy the exergue.

Bibliography: H. Hoffmann, *Ten Centuries that Shaped the West* (Houston 1971) 386-87. On the Gigantomachy: F. Vian, *La guerre de Géants* (Paris 1952). On the Peisistratid pediment: B. S. Ridgway, *The Archaic Style in Greek Sculpture* (Princeton 1977) 205-206. Segment Class: Beazley, *ABV* 212-214.

4

Attic Red-Figure Column-Krater

Collection of Gilbert M. Denman, Jr., San Antonio
Attributed to the Orchard Painter [Bothmer]
Ca. 470-460 B.C.
> Height: 44.2 cm.
> Diameter: 41 cm.

Side A:　Athena punishing the Daughters of Kekrops
Side B:　Youth and two women

In the Early Classical period, just after 480, a variety of stories relating to the mythical history of Athens began to appear in Attic red-figure. Among the early legendary kings of Attica, Erechtheus (also called Erichthonios) was popular with the vase-painters, especially the stories surrounding his birth. He was the child of Hephaistos and of Ge, the Earth, who took in his seed after Athena had rejected the god's advances. When the baby Erichthonios was born out of the earth, a scene depicted on several vases, Athena was present and took up the child as foster-mother. She put him in a chest, together with a guardian serpent to protect him, and entrusted the chest to the three daughters of Kekrops, instructing them not to open it. These three sisters, children of the first king of Attica, were named Aglauros, Herse, and Pandrosos. According to Pausanias (1.18.2), Pandrosos obeyed Athena's command, but her two sisters, overcome by curiosity, opened the chest. A slightly different version, attested by Ovid (*Metamorphoses* 2.558ff), holds that all three were at fault: Aglauros persuaded the other two to open the chest. In any event, the unfortunate sisters, horrified by the sight, were driven mad and jumped from the Acropolis.

On side A, Athena chastises the three sisters for disregarding her injunction. Two of the girls try to flee to the left, looking back at Athena, but the goddess takes hold of the nearer one by the shoulder. The third sister, presumably the obedient Pandrosos, observes the others as she moves off to the right. All three wear *chitons*, two of them finely pleated, and over them *himatia*. One wears a sakkos on her head, one a simple headband, and the third nothing at all. Athena is particularly splendidly dressed. Her *chiton* is embroidered with a three-dot pattern and has a wide hem decorated with leaping dolphins between borders of dots and parallel lines. The dotted border appears at the sleeves and at the neck as well. Over the *chiton* she wears a mantle with stiff folds, and her aegis is decorated with a stippled pattern, a dot border, nineteen snakes, and a comical Gorgoneîon. The cap of her Attic helmet is embellished with engraved spirals, and the low crest trails down over her shoulder. She carries a long spear in her left hand; the two girls at the left each carry a spiralling branch.

On side B, a youth stands between two muffled female figures who run off, looking back toward him. The

Side A

Side B

woman at the right is virtually identical to Pandrosos in dress and pose, though the drawing of the reverse is in general far less careful. The reverse also lacks the frieze of palmettes which decorates the neck on side A. The youth wields a stick with a T-shaped head with which he seems to be threatening one of the girls.

The story depicted on side A, Athena punishing the Kekropides, appears on only a few other vases, including a lekythos in Basel, an alabastron in Athens, and fragments from the Acropolis and in Leipzig. The Basel vase includes the chest and the snake, which are omitted from the Denman scene, but on all of these except the Leipzig vase only one of the sisters is shown. Thus this example is the only complete version showing Athena with all three daughters of Kekrops.

The Denman krater has been attributed by Dietrich von Bothmer to a painter of the Early Classical period who decorated a variety of larger shapes, but favored the column-krater. He is named for an unusual scene on a column-krater in New York showing women in an orchard, picking fruit (Beazley, *ARV*² 523,1). Though he is not generally known as a painter of interesting mythological scenes, there is one other from his hand, on a well known column-krater also in New York: Jason stealing the golden fleece (*ARV*² 524,28). As Bothmer points out, the gorgoneion on Athena's aegis on the Jason krater provides a good comparison with the peculiar gorgoneion on this vase.

Bibliography: *Kunst der Antike* (Gallerie Günter Puhze, Freiburg, 1981) no. 158. For other representations of Athena and the Kekropides: M. Schmidt, "Die Entdeckung des Erichthonios," *Mitteilungen des Deutschen Archaeologischen Instituts, Athenische Abteilung* 83 (1968) 200-212 and pl. 73-74 (Basel lekythos), pl. 76 (alabastron in Athens); U. Kron, *Die zehn attischen Phylenheroen* (Berlin 1976) 71-72 and pl. 2,2 (fragmentary vase in Leipzig); Beazley, *ARV*² 973, 7-8 (Acropolis fragments).

5

Attic Black-Figure Lekythos (White-Ground)

Collection of The University Museums, University of Mississippi Phase I Cultural
   Center (77.3.82)
Attributed to the Diosphos Painter
500-490 B.C.
   Height: 27.4 cm.
   Diameter: 9.9 cm.

Hermes and Iris

The winged messengers of Zeus, each carrying the herald's *kerykeion* (caduceus) and wearing a short *chiton* and winged boots, walk to the right in animated conversation. Perhaps they are discussing the box that dangles from Iris' left hand — a gift from Zeus to some mortal girl who has caught his fancy? Iris appears comparatively seldom in vase painting. Her name is the Greek word for the rainbow, and in popular fancy, the apearance of a rainbow was a sign that Zeus had sent Iris to earth with a message. There is no story here, however; the painter has merely given us a little vignette from the everyday life of the gods.

The technique of placing a black silhouette against a white background instead of a red one was a comparative novelty when this lekythos was painted (see [26]), and it must have looked very striking when it was whole and not discolored by fire. The "inscrip-tions" are nonsense, strings of T's and X's used simply to break up the space around the figures and make a pattern that links them visually to the intricate arrangement of palmettes on either side. There is a strong contrast between the careful organization of the abstract patterns and the spontaneity in the treatment of the figures, produced by the slapdash incision, the jaunty gesture of Hermes and the pert flip of Iris' *chiton*.

The Mississippi lekythos is attributed to the Diosphos Painter, a prolific painter of neck-amphoras [24] and lekythoi, in both conventional black-figure and white-ground techniques, as well as a technique called semi-outline. The latter is a transitional stage in the development toward outline drawing on a white ground [42-45]. This example, however, though on a white ground, is purely black-figure.

LUCY TURNBULL

Bibliography: *CVA* Robinson Collection 1, pl. 38, 7; C.H.E. Haspels, *Attic Black-figured Lekythoi* (Paris 1936), 111 and 235; Beazley, *Paralipomena* 248; D.C. Kurtz, *Athenian White Lekythoi* (Oxford 1975) 98 and fig. 28a (shoulder palmettes).

6

Attic Red-Figure Pelike

Collection of The University Museums, University of Mississippi, Phase I Cultural
  Center (77.3.196)
Attributed to the Washing Painter [Turnbull]
430-420 B.C.
    Height: 12 cm.
    Diameter: 10.9 cm.

Side A: Eros and girl
Side B: Youth with phiale

The young god of love floats toward the girl, holding two red balls, perhaps fruit or balls of wool. Nude except for the *sakkos* on her head, she holds a box in both hands, and stares at Eros. Between them on the floor is a *kalathos*, a basket containing folded cloth or skeins of wool. **On side B**, a young man holds a phiale, a type of cup used in pouring libations to the gods. Has he been making an offering to Eros?

Scenes of Eros and women together indoors become common in the late 5th century B.C. This Eros is not the embodiment of an irresistible power that not even Zeus can escape, but simply a charming adolescent boy who happens to have wings. Nor is he occupied with the loves of the immortal gods, but only visiting an anonymous mortal girl. The figure of Eros undergoes a curious change in the 5th century. In the beginning he is represented as a young man in miniature, but each generation of painters made him younger in appearance, perhaps in response to the erotic connotations of youthful male beauty in Athenian society. By the middle of the 4th century, the image had evolved of the chubby, mischievous winged baby, familiar to us under his Roman name of Cupid. Since she is naked, the girl must be a *hetaira*, a "companion" of the sort that entertained the guests at men's dinner parties. She is dressing to go out or to receive a client, and the chest she holds must contain clothes or jewelry. Eros here may be thought of as endowing her with greater beauty and sex appeal. The tone is light, rather trivial, mildly erotic, in keeping with the growing contemporary taste for scenes from the daily life of women.   LUCY TURNBULL

Bibliography: Unpublished. On Eros: A. Greifenhagen, *Griechische Eroten*
(Berlin 1957).

Side A

Side B

27

7

Etruscan Alabastron with Applied Color

Collection of The University Museums, University of Mississippi Phase I Cultural Center (1977.3.142)
Unattributed
Ca. 400 B.C.
   Height: 9.7 cm.
   Diameter: 3.2 cm.

Boreas pursuing a nymph

A nymph sprints away at top speed, long rubbery hands and feet outstretched. Her hair streams out behind her, and her flimsy *chiton* is pasted to her body by the speed at which she runs. Behind her Boreas, god of the north wind, comes sailing on big wings, his arms reaching out to catch her. An extra note of humor is added by the painter's choice of such a small cylindrical object on which to paint the scene; the nymph in her frantic flight almost trips over the heels of her pursuer. His name, ΒΟΡΕΑΣ is written below his arms; her name, partly obliterated by abrasion, is written from top to bottom in front of her body: ..ΙΑΝ .. Α — Deianeira? The drawing is in the style of the Meidias Painter and his followers in the last quarter of the 5th century B.C.

Boreas first appears in Attic vase-painting shortly after the Persian Wars, when the Athenians built him a shrine and paid him special honors in gratitude for the northerly storms that had destroyed a significant part of the Persian fleet. There was also a popular tradition that Boreas had fallen in love with an Athenian princess, Oreithyia, and had snatched her up in a storm of wind to be his wife. Vase-painters frequently represented this subject, but no Attic version is as broadly comic as this one. The wind god on Attic vases may look uncouth, the princess frightened, but they are never made undignified even in the latest works.

The technique too is not Attic. This is not true red-figure with figures reserved in the natural color of the clay; the figures are painted in yellowish-red paint (now discolored by fire) over the black glaze, with details incised with a sharp point so that the black shows through. This is an Etruscan technique, developed in imitation of Attic red-figure, which like the earlier black-figure ware was imported in very large quantities into Etruria. Etruscan painters had produced imitation black-figure too, and when the style changed they were evidently reluctant to give up the familiar incision technique. This compromise method lasts until the end of the 5th century. Etruscan painters often gave a humorous twist to Greek mythological subjects and altered the names of the persons involved. In fact only the style of the drawing on this alabastron looks Attic. The irreverent treatment of the subject and the altered name of the nymph, as well as the metallic luster of the glaze and the Etruscan technique, all suggest an Etruscan origin. This hypothesis is confirmed by a close inspection of the letter forms, which reveals that the N and E are not Greek, but Etruscan. A number of Athenian potters and painters emigrated to South Italy and Etruria in the last years of the 5th century, and it may be that one of them inspired the drawing on this vase.

LUCY TURNBULL

Bibliography: Unpublished. For Boreas and Oreithyia: S. Kaempf-Dimitriadou, *Die Liebe der Götter in der attischen Kunst des V. Jahrhunderts v. Chr.* (Bern 1979). For the technique: J.D. Beazley, *Etruscan Vase Painting* (Oxford 1947), ch. 12.

29

8

Attic Red-Figure Neck-Amphora with Twisted Handles

Collection of the John and Mable Ringling Museum of Art, Sarasota (1600. G2)
Attributed to the Harrow Painter
Ca. 470 B. C.
  Height: 27.7 cm.
  Diameter: 18.1 cm.

Side A: Running Nike with torches
Side B: Standing youth

The Harrow Painter, a competent late archaic pot painter, here follows the tradition established by his mentor, the Berlin Painter (see [63]), of placing one figure on either side of an otherwise completely black amphora. The more important figure on **side A** is a winged female wearing a *chiton* and *sakkos*. She is running along to the right on a rough groundline and is carrying a lighted torch in each hand, the flame indicated in red. She is one of the many manifestations of the Victory goddess Nike, in this instance probably hurrying to light an altar (cf. [9]).

The reverse shows a lone draped youth standing in profile to the right on a thin reserved groundline. The majority of amphorae by this painter have such a figure as a filling device on the less important back side of the vase. The Berlin Painter shows his influence here as well, since he often combined a Nike and anonymous youth in his later paintings.

JENIFER NEILS

Bibliography: Beazley, *ARV*² 272, 9. On late Nikai by the Berlin Painter:
C. Isler-Kerényi, "Ein Spätwerk des Berliner Malers," *Antike Kunst* 14 (1971) 25-31.

Side A

Side B

9

Attic Red-Figure Lekythos

Collection of The Archer M. Huntington Art Gallery, University of Texas, Austin (1980.63)
Attributed to the Oionokles Painter
Ca. 470 B.C.
Height: 36.5 cm.

Flying Nike with cithara and phiale

This charming lekythos shows a winged Victory hovering in mid-flight. Her progress is to the left, but momentarily checked, as she looks back to the right. Her ornate wings and her drapery, a *chiton* and diagonal mantle, flutter out behind. She wears a diadem in her flaxen hair, which is rolled up in back. Lightsome as this Nike is, she is burdened with heavy equipment: in her outstretched right hand she holds a plain phiale; in her left is cradled a large cithara or lyre, the strings of which are facing her. A dotted strap with trailing ends attaches the instrument to her left hand, and a long, fringed, diamond-patterned scarf is draped over her forearm. There is a nonsense inscription in the field under the wings. The picture is framed above and below by zones of stopped meander, and as is common on lekythoi of this period, palmettes decorate the shoulder.

The figure of Nike, while known earlier in Attic vase-painting, becomes especially prevalent after ca. 480 B.C., especially on smaller vases like Nolan amphorae and lekythoi. The victory she alludes to is not always known, unless she is accompanied by other figures, like warriors or athletes, or carries a specific attribute. Here, the presence of the cithara implies a victory in a musical competition. A Nolan amphora formerly in Goluchow by the same hand (Beazley, *ARV²* 646, 10) details the narrative more fully: a Nike with cithara on one side is presenting the instrument to a young citharode or lyre-player with outstretched hand on the other. While the musician is missing on the Austin lekythos, his presence is implied by the Nike's glance.

This painting represents an extremely fine work by the so-called Oionokles Painter, an early classic artist whose name derives from four *kalos* inscriptions. Beazley calls him a follower of the Providence Painter, who in turn was a pupil of the Berlin Painter [63], and both predecessors produced many pictures of Nike. However, the high quality of this work singles it out, and perhaps the same can be said of it, as Beazley said of an earlier lekythos with a cithara-bearing Nike by the Pan Painter (Oxford 312; Beazley, *ARV²* 556, 102), "a triumph of technique — pot, figure, patternwork." JENIFER NEILS

Bibliography: Unpublished. On Nike: C. Isler-Kerényi, *Nike: der Typus der laufenden Flügelfrau in archaischer Kunst* (Zurich, 1969). On cithara playing: J.D. Beazley, "Citharoedus," *Journal of Hellenic Studies* 42 (1922) 70-98. On the Oionokles Painter: Beazley, *ARV²* 646-649.

Dionysos and his Circle

Though not one of the twelve Olympians, Dionysos probably played a greater role in the everyday and religious life of the average Greek than any other divinity. This importance is borne out by his appearances on painted pottery, which far outnumber those of any other mythological figure. His popularity stemmed mainly from his gift of the grape and, through it, the opportunity for a release from the drudgery and worry of daily life.

Dionysos was a relative newcomer to the Greek pantheon, and many myths make it clear that he and his worship came into Greece from outside and not without resistance. Ultimately, this must be true of all the Olympians, since the earliest Greek speakers apparently entered the country only in the second millenium, and Dionysos' name does occur in Linear B tablets of the late Bronze Age (ca. 1400-1200 B.C.). It may be, then, that his cult was reintroduced in the early first millenium along with invasions from Thrace, and the memory of this is embodied in the myths. Homer, in the eight century, seems scarcely to be aware of Dionysos, but this is partly because the Olympian gods of Homeric religion are a product of aristocratic society in the late Iron Age, while Dionysos, along with Demeter, goddess of the grain, appealed mainly to the common man.

Most of the ancient sources, including the one Homeric passage that mentions him (*Iliad* 6.130 f.), associate Dionysos with Thrace, though some link him to Phrygia. Certainly his orgiastic cult would have been at home in the East. But the evidence for active worship of the god in Thrace and neighboring Macedonia in historical times argues strongly that this was his place of origin. Euripides' great play celebrating Dionysos' power, the *Bacchae*, was composed and first performed at the court of the Macedonian king.

All sources agree that Dionysos was the child of a mortal woman, Semele, and of Zeus. When the pregnant Semele was incinerated by beholding Zeus in full majesty, the fetus was saved and completed its gestation in the thigh of Zeus. This was the second time Zeus himself gave birth to one of his children (the first being Athena). Unable to care for the newborn, he entrusted it to Hermes, who in turn delivered the infant to the nymphs of Mount Nysa, in Thrace, to bring up. Thence the young god made his way to Greece.

The major centers of Dionysos' worship in Greece were Boeotia and Attica. How he established himself in Thebes, chief city of Boeotia, is the subject of Euripides' play. His popularity in Athens is underscored by the two major dramatic festivals held in the god's honor every year, which were perhaps the only occasions, apart from the Panathenaia, when all Athenian citizens gathered in one place. The earliest small temple of Dionysos, on the south slope of the Acropolis, where the later famous theatre of Dionysos would be built, belongs to the mid-sixth century.

Among the thousands of Dionysiac scenes on Attic vases, relatively few show a narrative subject. In addition to his birth and infancy, the god's encounter with a band of pirates whom he turned into dolphins is shown once, on a well-known cup by Exekias (Beazley, *ABV* 146, 21). Only one myth involving Dionysos is reasonably popular: the Return of Hephaistos, in which the lame god of the forge, whose mother Hera had thrown him from Olympos, is coaxed back by Dionysos' wine, accompanied by a rowdy procession.

Most of the time Dionysos is alone or with one or more members of his retinue: his consort Ariadne, the Cretan princess, whom the god found abandoned by Theseus on the island of Naxos; the maenads, his ecstatic women followers; and satyrs, who embody the animal nature which an excess of Dionysos' gift brings out in all of us. In Archaic and most of Classical art, Dionysos is portrayed as a mature and stately bearded figure, never seeming to be under the influence himself, usually recognized by his kantharos and ivy crown [14]. Only in late red-figure does he sometimes appear as the effete young dandy of Euripides' *Bacchae*. The maenads in historical times were ordinary housewives who periodically abandoned home and family to worship their god on a remote mountainside. On vases their conventional attributes are a fawn skin worn over a chiton [11] and a thyrsos, or fennel stalk, held aloft [16]. At their wildest they tore apart small animals and ate the flesh raw [16], but more often they look rather subdued and lack the traditional attire [12, 13]. Satyrs undergo a gradual transformation from early black-figure, when they are at their most bestial, sometimes hairy and misshapen [17], to classical red-figure, when they may be distinguishable from human males only by the tail, snub nose, and, often, erect phallos.

10

Attic Red-Figure Neck-Amphora with Lid

Collection of The University Museums, University of Mississippi Phase I Cultural
  Center (1977.3.87a-b)
Attributed to the Harrow Painter
490-480 B.C.

> Height: 40.4 cm. without lid
> Diameter: 23.5 cm.
> Height of lid: 14 cm.

Side A: Dionysos pursuing Ariadne
Side B: Companion of Ariadne, fleeing

When the Athenian hero Theseus came to Crete to rescue his companions from the man-eating Minotaur, he needed the help of King Minos' daughter Ariadne to find his way into and out of the impenetrable maze, the Labyrinth, in which the monster was confined. She gave him a golden crown to light his way, or in some versions of the story, a ball of thread; he tied one end of this to the entrance and unrolled it as he went in, then followed it back when he had killed the Minotaur. Ariadne sailed with him for Athens, expecting to become his bride, but he deserted her on the island of Naxos. There Dionysos saw her, fell in love and married her. The Athenians had a version of the story more flattering to their national hero: Theseus left Ariadne only because Dionysos, having fallen in love with her himself, compelled him to sail away without her.

Like some of his contemporaries, the Harrow Painter liked to concentrate the viewer's attention on the painted figures by isolating them against the black background without a decorative frame or other distracting ornament. This device also allowed the painter to experiment with the expression of complex emotions and psychological states by means of carefully chosen details and gestures, rather than with the broad, energetic pantomime used by many black-figure and early red-figure painters. Here, the pursuit is over almost before it has begun, without violence or panic. A mortal cannot resist the power of a god, but this god has refrained from using his full power; although his parted lips betray his emotion, he does not

seize the girl in his arms or struggle with her. He takes one stride forward and grasps her shoulder with his left hand, while with his right hand he gently touches her arm but does not yet clasp it with his fingers. She takes a single step away, her right hand stretched out to the god with an imploring gesture, her left hand fearfully clutching a small round object (a flower, or the ball of thread?) to her bosom. She seems more hesitant and bewildered than frightened; even before the god's hand closes on her wrist, she has begun to turn back toward him, lifting her eyes to his face and gravely meeting his gaze. Soon the faithless mortal lover will be forgotten.

The god is identified as Dionysos by his wreath of ivy leaves, and the identification of Ariadne is almost equally certain, since in vase painting Dionysos does not appear with any other identifiable female figure. The companion of Ariadne on the reverse is not given any name; such fleeing companions are standard figures in scenes of gods or heroes pursuing women, and the painter of this amphora was not much interested in her. He has drawn her much more loosely than the main figures, with less attention to the details of clothing and jewelry, and her gesture is entirely conventional.

The Harrow Painter, to whom this vase is attributed, is one of the better Late Archaic and Early Classical painters of large pots, a follower of the Berlin Painter (see [8]).

LUCY TURNBULL

Bibliography: CVA Robinson Collection 2, Pl. 29,2; Beazley, ARV² 272, 2; S. Kämpf-Dimitriadou, *Die Liebe der Götter in der attischen Kunst des 5. Jahrhunderts v. Chr.* (Bern 1979), 30-31; 101, #305.

Side A   Side B

11

Attic Black-Figure Column-Krater

Collection of the Dallas Museum of Fine Arts,
    Gift of the Jonsson Foundation and Mr. and Mrs. Frederick M. Mayer (1972.22)
Unattributed
560-550 B. C.
        Height: 44 cm.
        Diameter: 53 cm.

Sides A and B: Dionysiac revelry

The main scene (**side A**) carries a boisterous group of dancing satyrs and maenads who cluster about a single bearded male figure. The revelers are the companions of Dionysos who is recognizable as the central, clad figure holding a drinking horn in his left hand. The reverse scene (**side B**) displays a single male figure clad in a robe similar to that of Dionysos. He is flanked by two pieces of cloth, which seem to float mystically in midair but are meant to be draped over pegs on the wall, and in turn by two heraldically placed lions with flicking tails and reversed heads. Under each handle a great bird in flight separates the two scenes. Bearded male heads adorn the handle-plates on the vase rim, itself decorated with wavy lines which recall the rippling action created by stirring the vase's contents.

Dionysiac revelries were popular subjects on Attic vases of the mid sixth century B. C. As seen here the satyrs and maenads gesticulate wildly, drawing the inspiration for their ecstatic mood from Dionysos, the god of ecstasy and abandonment of the rational. The frenzied mood of the revelers, however, is contrasted with the sedate and restrained pose of Dionysos himself. The direction of Dionysos' slow pace indicates a movement of the group to the right with the god in the center of his fold. Such scenes are not infrequently expanded to include the returning outcast, Hephaistos, being led back to Olympos by Dionysos. The Dallas vase does not include an image of the lame god, but the arrangement of Dionysos and his companions on the obverse, the vase's shape, and its date all invite comparison with the well known column-krater by Lydos in New York (Beazley, *ABV* 108, 5)

Both Lydos and the painter of this vase elected to place Dionysos in the center of his entourage on the obverse scene. While Lydos has depicted Hephaistos in a similar setting on the reverse of the New York krater, thus creating the effect of a continuous movement around the entire vase, this painter has effectively curtailed the impression of a procession by turning the attention of three lead characters back toward Dionysos. Their reverse action focuses our attention on the god and successfully permits the composition of the scene to be complete in itself.

The soaring birds in the handle zones and the wild creatures on the reverse of the Dallas krater are also familiar Lydan traits. While the painter elected to depict a human between the lions instead of the more common choice of an animal of a different species, he has attempted to segregate the central figure from the snarling beasts by inserting a row of vertical dots on either side of him.

While the painted style is purely Attic, the bold use of animals in a major scene, the extensive use of color, the dotted lions' manes, and dotted rosettes in the field all testify to a liberal incorporation of Corinthian motifs and practices. These, likewise, are typically Lydan.

KARL KILINSKI II

Bibliography: *Gazette des Beaux-Arts, La Chronique des Arts*, No. 1249 (February, 1973) 103, no. 367, *On View, A Guide to Museum and Gallery Acquisitions in Great Britian and America*, London: Plaiston Publications, 1974 edition; vol. 8, plate 247, p. 79. On Lydos: Beazley *ABV* 107ff; M. Tiverios, *Ho Lydos kai to Ergo tou* (Athens 1976).

Side A

Side B

12

Attic Black-Figure Neck Amphora

Collection of the Cummer Gallery of Art, Jacksonville
Group of Toronto 305
Ca. 520-510 B.C.
      Height: 40.6 cm.

Side A: Dionysos between dancing satyrs
Side B: Maenads

On side A, Dionysos stands in a rigid, statuesque pose, while two bearded satyrs dance about him. The god wears a long *chiton* with a pattern on the hem and, over it, a *himation*. His beard is long and thick, like those of the satyrs, and an ivy wreath crowns his head. He holds up a large kantharos in his left hand and a vine with three long tendrils in his right. The satyr at left wears a white ribbon hung from his right shoulder across his chest.

On side B, a group of women stands aligned in an orderly row. At left and right is an overlapping pair standing side by side; the woman in the center appears to be alone, though it is possible that she too has a companion, completely hidden from view, as Beazley assumed, for a total of six. All are dressed alike in embroidered *chiton* and *himation*, and all wear a fillet, with long tresses falling behind and over the shoulder.

Two carry a pair of castanets (*krotala*), and the woman in the center holds a spreading vine. Though they have none of the identifying attributes of maenads - animal skin, thyrsos - the presence of Dionysos on the other side leads us to suppose that they are his followers.

A small frieze of lions and boars runs beneath the figured scene, a feature more common on hydrias of this period than on amphoras.

This vase is one of a large number of amphoras and hydrias of the late sixth century related to the circle of the Antimenes Painter, the most prolific artist of the years ca. 530 - 510 (see [37]). Among several groups distinguished by Beazley, the Group of Toronto 305 includes about 20 amphoras, most of them with a Dionysiac subject. Only one other, in Sydney (Beazley, *ABV* 283, 8*bis*), includes the animal frieze.

Bibliography: Beazley, *Paralipomena* 125, 5*bis*; Sale Catalogue, Christie's London, April 28, 1964. Lot. 65, pl. 10.

Side A

Side B

13

Attic Black-Figure Eye-Cup

Collection of Mr. and Mrs. Edward L. Diefenthal, Metairie, Louisiana
Attributed to the Krokotos Group [Cahn]
Ca. 520 B.C.

Height: 11.5 cm.
Diameter (without handles): 29 cm.

Interior: Gorgoneion
Side A: Dionysos and Ariadne, between eyes
Side B: Dionysos and two maenads, between eyes

On both sides of the exterior, Dionysos stands to the right, holding up a rhyton in his left hand. He wears a *chiton* and, over it, a striped *himation* with a decoration of stippled rosettes. He has an ivy wreath in his hair and a long pointy beard. **On side A**, a woman stands in profile to left, facing the god and gesturing with her right hand. She wears a *chiton* decorated with an incised scale pattern and a striped *himation*. Since she is alone with Dionysos, she is probably to be identified as Ariadne, the Cretan princess who became the god's consort after he discovered her on the island of Naxos, abandoned there by Theseus.

On side B, the god is accompanied by two women who stand symmetrically on either side of him. They are dressed like Ariadne and make the same gesture of greeting. They may be unidentified goddesses or, more likely, maenads without the thyrsos or other attributes. Under and around each handle grow clusters of grapes hanging from vines. The vines continue around the eyes and the figural groups, and directly under each handle is a pair of intertwining branches.

The eyes, for which this type of cup is named, first occur ten to fifteen years before this example, on Exekias' famous cup in Munich (Beazley, *ABV* 146, 21). They regularly occupy this position, next to the handles, allowing room for only a single figure or a small group between them. Though tremendously popular in this period, the eyes' true purpose or meaning is not entirely clear (see [28]).

The tondo, as often in eye-cups, is black and decorated in the center with a bearded Gorgon's head painted in outline, rather than black-figure.

The Diefenthal cup is probably a product of the large Krokotos workshop, which comprises several groups of eye-cups, one of which is the Group of Walters 48.22 [28]. Krokotos refers to the saffron yellow used by some painters of the workshop for animals and garments. Dietrich von Bothmer suggests that this cup may be by the same hand as one in Mannheim (Cg38; *CVA* pl. 17).

Bibliography: Unpublished. Krokotos Group: Beazley, *ABV* 205-208.

Side A

Side B

Interior

43

14

Attic Black-Figure Neck-Amphora

Collection of The Lowe Art Museum, University of Miami, Coral Gables,
   Anonymous Gift (56.001.000)
Unattributed
520-500 B.C.
   Height: 37.5 cm.
   Diameter: 28 cm.

Side A: Dionysos with satyrs and maenads
Side B: Warrior in a wheeling chariot

Most black-figure scenes of Dionysos emphasize his role as giver of the gift of wine. **On side A**, two large bunches of grapes hang prominently from vines in the background. The god himself, in the center, holds a kantharos, the wine vessel most closely associated with him, and one of the satyrs holds an oinochoe with high-swung handle, used for serving wine. Dionysos wears an ivy crown and a *himation* over a long *chiton*. Both garments are decorated with dots forming diamond patterns, and a row of dots adorns the hem of the *chiton*.

The god is framed by two symmetrical pairs of a satyr and a maenad. Often maenads are seen fending off the advances of aroused satyrs, but here the couples are on rather friendly terms, as they stand side by side and casually embrace. It looks as if the influence of the wine may have made the maenads more amenable than usual. Each is dressed in a belted *chiton* decorated in the same manner as Dionysos' garments.

Side B shows a four horse chariot wheeling around, an especially popular motif on later black-figure neck-amphoras [48]. The driver is a warrior in a low crested Corinthian helmet. He carries several spears and a shield, facing the viewer, which has as its device three white balls. Another shield appears to rest on the warrior's back and is seen in profile.

Bibliography: unpublished.

Side A

Side B

15

Attic Black-Figure Skyphos

Collection of the New Orleans Museum of Art
CHC Group
Ca. 500 B. C.
    Height: 14.7 cm.
    Diameter: 22.5 cm.

Side A: Dionysos between satyrs and maenads
Side B: The like

The skyphos is a drinking vessel, and the ample proportions of this example would have contained a rather generous serving of wine. The Dionysiac subject matter is in keeping with the vase's function.

On both sides, Dionysos occupies the center of a nearly perfectly symmetrical composition. He stands in profile to the right, holding up a large rhyton in his left hand. The god wears a striped mantle and an ivy wreath in his hair. On either side of him stands a nude satyr, each facing the god, with one hand raised in greeting. Moving outward, next come two maenads also looking toward the center. They wear belted *chitons*, and on two of the four, incised lines suggest an animal hide tied over the *chiton*. The whole group is framed by a pair of crouching sphinxes facing outward. A large palmette occupies the space between handles and sphinxes.

Bibliography: Beazley, *ABV* 620, 88; Louis P. di Cesnola, *A Descriptive Atlas of the Cesnola Collection of Cypriote Antiquities in the Metropolitan Museum of Art, New York* (Boston and New York 1885-1903) ii pl. 148, 1099; *Cypriote and Classical Antiquities, Duplicates of the Cesnola and other Collections*, Sale Catalogue, Anderson Galleries, New York, 30-31 March, 1928, i, 107, 395.

Side A

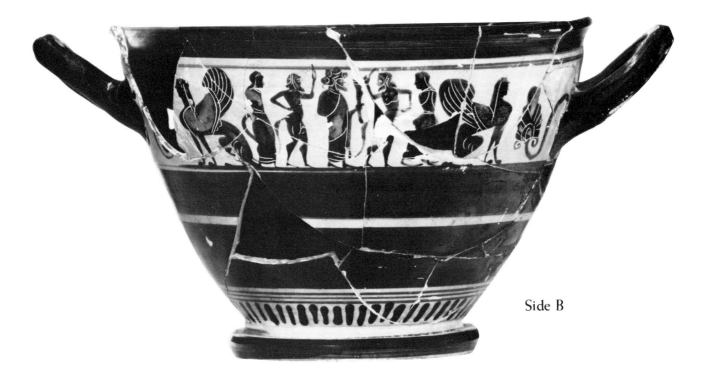

Side B

16

Attic Black-Figure Neck-Amphora

Collection of The University Museums, University of Mississippi, Phase I
 Cultural Center (77.3.58)
Attributed to the Diosphos Painter
 510-500 B.C.
 Height: 20.1 cm.
 Diameter: 11.3 cm.

Side A: Dionysos, satyr and maenad
Side B: Two maenads with wild animals

Red beard wagging briskly, both feet off the ground, the satyr **on side A** leaps upon the maenad as if to bring her down with a flying tackle. She holds her thyrsos in one hand and extends the other toward Dionysos, begging for help, but the god merely stands and watches. Dionysos was not simply a god of wine; he was a fertility god as well, as the celebrations of the Country Dionysia in Attic villages made clear. Enormous images of human genitalia were carried in procession through the streets, to the accompaniment of obscene jokes and songs. In its primitive beginnings the custom was probably meant to stimulate, by this example, the plants and vines to grow and be fruitful. Even at the more sophisticated City Dionysia, where the god was honored with dramatic presentations, this phallic element was retained in the grotesquely padded costumes and uninhibited obscenity of comedy. In art, the phallic aspect of Dionysos' cult is represented by the satyrs with their half-animal appearance and their extravagant lecherousness. Earlier black-figure painting has some scenes of actual copulation between satyrs and maenads in which the maenads seem to be cooperating enthusiastically, but this amphora shows a more dignified encounter: the maenad tried to escape but does not defend herself very energetically.

Later, in the early 5th century, maenads are shown using the thyrsos to hold off attacking satyrs, whose approaches are usually more cautious than the one here, and by the end of the century the subject had gone out of fashion.

Side B shows another aspect of Dionysiac cult. Two maenads are dancing in an ecstatic trance; possessed by the spirit of the god, they can perform superhuman feats of strength, are impervious to weapons and can handle wild animals and poisonous snakes without harm. Here, one carries a deer on her shoulders and the other dangles a young lion by its tail. The moment is approaching the *sparagmos*, the climactic act of communion with the god, when they will tear the animals to pieces with their bare hands and eat the raw flesh. These maenads are to be considered nymphs rather than contemporary mortal worshipers, but this violent form of Dionysiac cult continued to be practiced in Thrace, and possibly in some parts of Greece, in the Classical period.

This vase is attributed to the Diospos Painter, a prolific painter of late black-figure lekythoi and neck-amphoras (see [24]).

LUCY TURNBULL

Bibliography: CVA Robinson Collection 1, pl. 30,1; Beazley, *Paralipomena*, 248; C. H. E. Haspels, *Attic Black-figured Lekythoi* (Paris 1936), 239, #136. For Dionysos and his cult: W. Otto, *Dionysos, Myth and Cult* (Indiana 1965).

Side A

Side B

17

Attic Black-Figure Oinochoe (White-Ground)

Collection of the John and Mable Ringling Museum of Art, Sarasota (1600.G5)
Workshop of the Athena Painter
Ca. 500-480 B.C.
    Height: 23.8 cm.
    Diameter: 41.9 cm.

Two travelling satyrs

Satyrs are so prevalent on Attic vases that they often appear on their own in a variety of scenes where we might have expected the presence of Dionysos. This pair looks like an excerpt from a lively procession accompanying the god.

The satyr at left rides on a goat with long curving horns and a long beard. The satyr wears a wide-brimmed traveller's hat, the *petasos*, and carries a rhyton in his raised right hand. He is also dressed in a short-sleeved *chiton* and a *himation* across his lap. He sits backwards on the animal, his feet dangling on either side, and turns to look ahead. In front a chubby satyr walks slowly as he plays the double flutes. He is nude but for a fillet in his hair, and the flute case hangs from his elbow. The fleshy folds of his belly are marked by incised lines, and his tail is particularly full, both perhaps signs of advancing age. A vine pattern criss-crosses the background.

The white-ground technique, that is, the application of a thick layer of creamy white to the clay surface before decorating with figures in black glaze, had been experimented with first about 525. Its use was popularized by the Edinburgh Painter, starting about 500 and primarily on lekythoi [26], then spread almost immediately to oinochoai and a few other small shapes.

The Athena Painter was a slightly younger follower of the Edinburgh Painter who eagerly took up the latter's innovative use of white ground for lekythoi and oinochoai. He appears to have been the chief artist in a rather large workshop, and it is not always possible to say if a particular vase, such as the Ringling example, is from his own hand or that of a closely associated painter. The style of the Athena Painter is very close to that of a red-figure lekythos Painter, the Bowdoin Painter [52], and it is possible that they are one and the same artist, working in different techniques at different stages of his career.

Bibliography: Beazley *ABV* 527,17 and *Paralipomena* 264. On the Athena and Bowdoin Painters: D. C. Kurtz, *Athenian White Lekythoi* (Oxford 1975) 15-16.

18

Attic Red-Figure Miniature Lekythos

Collection of Mr. and Mrs. Edward L. Diefenthal, Metairie, Louisiana
Unattributed
450-400 B. C.
> Height: 15 cm.

Satyr at a fountain

Although the shape and ornament of this vase are commonplace (a secondary lekythos with meander and rays), the scene depicted on it is unusual if not unique. Crouching before an outdoor fountain is a nude figure with equine ears and tail, a satyr. Like most satyrs in Greek art he has a receding hairline, long, ragged beard, snub nose and large phallus. Behind him is his abandoned wine amphora garlanded with ivy. The fountain consists of a masonry structure with an animal head spout. While Greek fountains are usually equipped with feline head spouts, this one, with its stippled hair, heavy lower jaw and pointed ears, appears more canine or porcine in form; perhaps it represents a caricature of a lion head. Thin strokes of paint emerging from the spout and crossing the satyr's extended left arm are no doubt streams of water. Thus, it looks as if the satyr has paused in his heated revelries to take a refreshing shower. In the late sixth and early fifth centuries B. C., the performance of satyr plays in Athens prompted the depiction of many genre-like scenes of satyrs, such as domestic life and athletics. While this reading of the scene would make it unique in Attic vase-painting, another interpretation is possible.

Mythological sources tell of one particular satyr, Silenos, being ambushed and taken to King Midas. His capture, which took place at a fountain, was facilitated by mixing wine with the water and thus inebriating the susceptible satyr. The most common representation of the myth shows the bound Silenos being led away; a few others show his ambush at the fountain. In the latter case, Silenos is clearly drinking from the spout while his captors crouch nearby. Since the Diefenthal lekythos shows neither the captors nor Silenos drinking, the mythological interpretation of the scene is not assured. In either case, however, the vase is an unusual and engaging piece.

JENIFER NEILS

Bibliography: Unpublished. On satyrs: F. Brommer, *Satyrspiele* (Berlin, 1944). On the capture of Silenos: F. Brommer, "Midassage," *Archäologischer Anzeiger* 1941, 36-52; idem, *Vasenlisten*[3], 534-535.

19

Attic Red-Figure Cup

Collection of The University Museums, University of Mississippi Phase I
  Cultural Center (1977.3.103)
Attributed to the Bonn Painter [Robinson]
Ca. 510 B.C.
  Height: 7 cm.
  Diameter (with handles): 23 cm.

Interior: Satyr with rhyton and column-krater

The satyr, ithyphallic as usual in early red-figure painting, crouches beside an enormous column krater. His right hand, concealed by the rim of the krater, is dipping out wine to fill his rhyton, a drinking cup made from an animal's horn. He wears a red fillet with tassels or flowers over his bald head and horsy ears. To the left of his head, the name ΛΕΑΓΡΟΣ (Leagros) is written from right to left.

As companion of Dionysos, the satyr is an appropriate ornament for a cup; this is one of many grotesque or obscene pictures drawn on the interior of cups, where their emergence as the wine level sank might startle or amuse the drinker. Half animal, half human in appearance, satyrs are spirits of uninhibited sensuality, perpetually drunk, perpetually lustful, totally without intellect (one early poet called them "unemployable loafers"). Their animal nature is indicated by their appearance, with horse tails, ears like pigs or horses, piggy snub noses and bald heads (baldness in antiquity was considered a sign or virility) and, in early black-figure, shaggy coats of hair all over their bodies. In vase painting their chief occupations are drinking, dancing, flute playing and sexually assaulting maenads, goats, goddesses and occasionally each other. In later red-figure, satyrs appear tamer; the maenads ward off their attacks without much trouble, and they begin to appear in scenes of ritual, where it is clear that the women involved are not spirits of nature but human women, and the satyrs behave more quietly. In the later 5th century a new type of satyr appears, youthful, with a more human face and a full head of hair, as well as better manners.

The name Leagros on this cup does not belong to the satyr but to a young Athenian contemporary of aristocratic birth. The Greeks set a very high value on physical beauty, counting it almost as a virtue in itself, and certainly a quality whose lack somehow diminished even an otherwise admirable person. In a society which approved and encouraged homosexual love affairs between men and youths, the beauty of adolescent boys was admired most of all. A particularly attractive boy could become a popular sensation, courted by many wooers, celebrated by poets and even by vase painters, who would inscribe his name on their products, either by itself or with the adjective *kalos* — "beautiful." A very few of these inscribed vases may have been commissioned as gifts or keepsakes, but for the most part the painters must simply have been trying to add a note of fashion and aristocratic elegance to their wares. The Leagros of this cup must have been outstandingly lovely, for his name appears on more than 60 surviving vases.

LUCY TURNBULL

Bibliography: *CVA* Robinson Collection 2, pl. 3,1. Beazley, ARV² 1593, 38. For satyrs: F. Brommer, *Satyroi* (Würzburg 1937).

Herakles

Most beloved of all Greek heroes, Herakles was the subject of innumerable myths chronicling his life and deeds from a precocious infancy to sudden death and apotheosis. He was the object of cult worship in every part of the Greek world, from Spain to the Levant, and the chief inspiration for ancient artists from Geometric Greece to the Roman Empire.

Herakles is scarcely mentioned in Homer, and early epic poems which must have been composed about him are now lost. Therefore both ancient mythographers and modern scholars have had to piece together his long and eventful career from many disparate sources. He was born to a mortal woman, Alkmene, who had conceived him by the god Zeus, impersonating her husband, King Amphitryon of Thebes. Other myths link Herakles with the Bronze Age site of Tiryns, in the Argolid, and, unlike other Greek heroes, he is not closely tied to any one particular region. Rather, he is the only truly panhellenic hero, and his worship was strongest in some areas, such as Attica, with which he had relatively little mythological connection. Herakles is unique in a second respect: though regarded as a mortal man and, like other offspring of such "mixed marriages" between a god and a mortal woman, subject to death, he nevertheless rose from his funeral pyre on Mount Oeta, in Thessaly, to become a god and live among the divinities on Mount Olympos. There he married the goddess Hebe and was thereby reconciled with her mother, Hera, who had plagued him throughout his life because he was the result of one of Zeus' adulterous affairs.

The centerpiece of Herakles' career is the twelve labors which he performed at the command of the Delphic Oracle, in servitude to his cousin Eurystheus, to expiate a murder. After the first labor, the killing of the Nemean Lion [20, 21], he skinned the beast and wore the hide, his most easily recognized attribute in Greek vase-paintings. The next several labors kept Herakles in the Peloponnesos and mostly involved the killing or capture of various animals. Then he went further afield, to capture the Cretan Bull [23], and finally travelled much further, to the Garden of the Hesperides, for the golden apples, and to the Underworld, to fetch the dog Kerberos. In the course of these travels he performed many incidental deeds, the *parerga*, such as the slaying of Triton [22] and of Kyknos [24].

Though most familiar to us as a man of action, Herakles is often depicted in quieter moments. He enjoyed some of the finer things in life, especially wine [28] and the company of women, though this side of his nature is seldom seen on vases. Even before his apotheosis he is not infrequently shown together with a god or goddess, usually Athena or Hermes [27].

Herakles had a rather stormy marital life. His first marriage, to the Theban princess Megara, ended when the hero was driven mad by Hera and murdered the couple's children. His second wife was Deianeira, from Kalydon in Aitolia, who was more faithful to him than he to her. Yet she unwittingly caused the hero's death because of his infidelity, deceived as she was by the dying centaur Nessos [25]. But the story of Herakles' death in an agony of pain has a happy ending, when his immortal soul ascends to Olympos, guided by the goddess who had always stood by him in life, Athena [26].

All of Herakles' labors were depicted in Attic vase-painting, with the exception of the sixth, the cleaning of the Augeian stables, and several appeared on Corinthian vases of the seventh and early sixth century before they entered the Athenian artists' repertoire. Several of the *parerga* occur even more often than some of the labors. Generally speaking Herakles is more popular in Attic black-figure than in red, and it has recently been suggested that the reason for his inordinate popularity on Attic vases of the Archaic period was a deliberate identification of the hero with the Athenian tyrant Peisistratos (see J. Boardman, in *Revue Archéologique* 1972, 57-72).

20

Attic Black-Figure Oinochoe

Collection of the Archer M. Huntington Art Gallery, the University of Texas,
    Austin, James R. Dougherty, Jr. Foundation and Archer M. Huntington
    Museum Fund Purchase (1980.33)
Related to the Class of Vatican G47
520-500 B.C.
    Height: 13.9 cm.

Herakles wrestling the Nemean Lion

The first of Herakles' labors was the capture and killing of the lion which had ravaged the valley around Nemea, in the northeastern Peloponnesos. The lion's invulnerable pelt rendered all weapons useless and forced the hero to engage the beast in a wrestling match and finally strangle it. Herakles skinned the dead animal and thereafter wore the impervious hide for protection, and in vase-painting it is usually his distinguishing attribute (see for example [27]).

On this vase, the wrestling match is in full swing and the outcome is still in doubt. Herakles is entirely nude, but for a fillet around his head and a baldric worn diagonally around his chest, to support a sword. His bow, quiver, and sword all rest in the branches of a tree in the background. With his left hand the hero is grasping the lion's belly, while his right holds off a rear paw with which the lion tries to claw Herakles' head. He hunches over the lion's luxuriant mane, leaving his thigh and groin area exposed and danger-ously close to the lion's open jaws. Behind Herakles stands Iolaos, his young nephew and frequent companion in his labors. He wears a corselet over a short *chiton* and holds Herakles' knotty club. His sword hangs from a baldric, and a second baldric crosses in an X pattern. He stretches out his left hand over the wrestling pair as a weak gesture of fright, or of encouragement for the hero.

In early black-figure, before about 540, Herakles and the lion regularly wrestle standing up. The great master Exekias apparently first showed them wrestling on the ground, as John Boardman has recently demonstrated, on a vase, fragments of which are at Ensérune. After that this version became increasingly popular in the last quarter of the sixth century, the period of the Austin oinochoe.

This vase is similar in shape to a large class of late sixth century oinochoai designated by Beazley the Class of Vatican G47. The term 'class' refers to shape and proportions, not to drawing style.

Bibliography: Beazley, *ABV* 431,9; Brommer, *Vasenlisten* [3] 136,40; *CVA* Castle Ashby (Great Britain 15) 13-14 and pl. 22.5-7; *Greek, Etruscan and South Italian Vases from Castle Ashby* Sale Catalogue, Christie's, London, July 2, 1980, lot. 78, p. 119, ill. On Herakles and the Lion: F. Brommer, *Herakles: die 12 Taten des Helden in der antiker Kunst und Literatur* (Cologne 1974) 7-11; for the wrestling match on the ground and the Ensérune fragments: J. Boardman, in *American Journal of Archaeology* 82 (1978) 14-15.

21

Attic Black-Figure Cup

Collection of Mrs. Nathan Polmer, New Orleans
Attributed to a Painter of the Leafless Group [Bothmer]
Ca. 500-480 B.C.

Height: 6.9 cm.
Diameter (without handles): 15.8 cm.

Interior: Running Satyr
Side A: Herakles wrestling the Nemean Lion
Side B: The like

The same scene is repeated without variation on both sides of the exterior. A nude Herakles leans over the charging lion, restraining it by grasping the left rear paw with his right hand. The hero's sword can be seen on the far side, as if projecting from his chest. The wrestlers are framed by a symmetrical pair of crouching youths, each with a cloak draped over his left arm. Both face to the right but look back left, so that only one observes the wrestling match. **On side A**, the artist has placed the wrestling pair off center, leaving too little room for the youth at left, who overlaps the handle. Hastily drawn trees and vines fill the background, and from one hangs Herakles' garment. A leaping dolphin appears under each handle. Though the draughtsmanship is rather careless and the incision minimal, the vitality of the struggle is effectively captured.

In the tondo, a satyr within a small reserved circle runs to the right, looking back. He has a thick fillet hung from his right arm and carries a large rhyton in his right hand. The vase did not fire properly in the tondo, probably because several were stacked one upon the other in the kiln. Thus the satyr appears dark red instead of black.

Bibliography: Brommer, *Vasenlisten*³ 135, A31. Leafless Group: Beazley, *ABV* 632-53 and *Paralipomena* 310-313; for the Polmer cup, Bothmer compares one on the Milan market (*Paralipomena* 312, bottom) and one at the University of Illinois (CM 135).

Side A

Side B

Interior

61

22

Attic Black-Figure Amphora

Collection of the New Orleans Museum of Art, Gift of Alvin P. Howard (16.39, formerly 2035)
Unattributed
Ca. 520-500 B.C.

Height: 28.6 cm.
Diameter: 17.5 cm.

Side A: Herakles battling Triton
Side B: Warrior and old men

Herakles' combat with the sea monster Triton (**side A**) is a favorite subject on Attic vases of the second half of the sixth century - this despite the fact that it is not one of the twelve labors and is in fact an episode completely unknown to the literary sources. Triton is mentioned by Hesiod (*Theogony* 930-33) as a son of Poseidon and Amphitrite, though not as an opponent of Herakles.

The scene should be distinguished from that of Herakles' struggle with another sea creature, Nereus, from whom the hero learned the way to the Garden of the Hesperides. That struggle is depicted on several early black-figure vases: Herakles is unarmed and Nereus is recognized by his ability to change his form into that of any animal or object and thus elude Herakles' grasp. A lion's head growing from his back or snakes held in his hands allude to the transformations. Nereus is a benign creature, the *Halios Geron* (Old Man of the Sea), only reluctant to divulge information. Triton is dangerous, and with him it is a fight to the death.

Herakles' battle with Triton replaces the struggle with Nereus on Attic vases rather abruptly soon before the mid-sixth century and then remains steadily popular until about 510. Triton's identity, in the absence of poetic sources, is established by several inscribed vases. The scene is confined to black-figure, apart from two red-figure exceptions.

The New Orleans example is typical of many others. Herakles wears his lion skin and carries a quiver over his shoulder, but his weapon is the sword. Triton puts up little resistance to the hero's onslaught. The join between human torso and fishy tail is at about the waist; the scales are small and the underside of the tail is marked by a thick line of white. An old man, balding and with white beard, watches from the left. This is probably none other than Nereus, who, after losing his monstrous form and then giving way to Triton on the vases, sometimes appears as an impartial witness to the combat.

On side B, a fully armed warrior sits on a low stool or bench. He wears a Corinthian helmet, and his sword is visible behind the round shield whose device is a quiver. He is flanked by two old men in *chiton* and *himation*, both with receding white hair and beard. The man at left moves off with a long stride, gesturing farewell with a raised hand. The other stays and faces the warrior, holding a staff. The scene is probably of epic inspiration, but the figures cannot be identified.

Bibliography: Brommer, *Vasenlisten* ³ 146, A18. On Triton: S. B. Luce, "Herakles and the Old Man of the Sea," *American Journal of Archaeology* 26 (1922) 174-92; R. Glynn, "Herakles, Nereus and Triton: a Study of Iconography in Sixth Century Athens," *Ibid.* 85 (1981) 121-32.

Side A

Side B

23

Attic Black-Figure Neck-Amphora

Collection of The University Museums, University of Mississippi Phase I
   Cultural Center (1977.3.61a-b)
Near the Antimenes Painter [Robinson]
530-520 B.C.

   Height: 41.6 cm.
   Diameter: 27.7 cm.
   Height of lid: 8 cm.

Side A: Herakles and the Cretan Bull
Side B: Hermes, Dionysos and goddess

Herakles' later labors carried him to the ends of the earth and beyond it to the land of the dead. By about the middle of the 6th century B.C. vase-painters were illustrating these exotic adventures, of which the capture of the Cretan Bull was one. King Minos of Crete, preparing to sacrifice to Poseidon, found he had no suitable victim. He prayed to the god, who sent a beautiful bull from the sea — so beautiful that Minos thought it too fine to sacrifice and kept it for himself. (Poseidon's revenge for this insult was to make Minos' wife fall in love with the bull; their son was the man-bull, the Minotaur.) Herakles' seventh labor was to capture and bring back this bull for his cowardly master Eurystheus. Unlike other animals Herakles encountered, the bull seems to have no supernatural qualities or other unusually dangerous abilities, and he captures it, in vase-painting at least, with relatively little difficulty. Here he has roped it around the horns and front legs, and it collapses at his feet. Hermes waits at left to guide the far-wandering hero back to Argos. This is not the most dramatic or fantastic of Herakles' adventures, but it was a favorite with black-figure painters; more than 140 examples are known.

In the center of **side B** stands Dionysos, turning his head to look at Hermes. At right stands a goddess holding on her shoulders two small children drawn, as always in archaic art, as miniature adults. None of the figures is named, but the two gods are recognizable because of the system of attributes — clothing, objects, gestures — by which even foreigners and illiterates could identify the personages depicted. Herakles' club, bow and lionskin cloak, or any one or combination of them, is sufficient to identify him. The same is true of Hermes' winged boots and herald's staff, or Dionysos' wreath, grapevine and cup. The goddess is more difficult to identify, though her general nature is clear: she is a *kourotrophos*, a goddess of fertility (not necessarily a mother goddess as such) who grants children to mankind, protects and nurtures them. The concept of such a goddess was already ancient among the Greeks when this amphora was painted, and it had become extremely complex and confused. In Athens and Attica "Kourotrophos" was a cult title of several goddesses, from Ge the Earth-Mother to virginal Artemis and Athena. Kourotrophos was also the name of a goddess or goddesses worshiped independently in shrines of their own, and Kourotrophos was honored by a preliminary sacrifice at major Athenian festivals. The goddess here wears an ivy wreath like Dionysos', and it may be that she is his wife Ariadne in the role of Kourotrophos, with their sons Staphylos and Oinopion. What it all meant to the wealthy Etruscan who bought this amphora and took it to his grave is impossible to guess.

LUCY TURNBULL

Bibliography: D.M. Robinson, "Unpublished Greek Vases in the Robinson Collection," *American Journal of Archaeology* 60 (1956), 1-25, pl. 4. Brommer, *Vasenlisten*[3] 195, A28. For Herakles and the Bull in archaic art: K. Schefold, *Götter- und Heldensagen der Griechen in der spätarchaischen Kunst* (Munich 1978) 103-105; for Kourotrophos: T. Hadzisteliou-Price, *Kourotrophos* (Leiden 1978)

Side A

Side B

24

Attic Black-Figure Neck-Amphora

Collection of the Virginia Museum of Fine Arts, Richmond, The Williams
    Fund (60-11)
Attributed to the Diosphos Painter
Ca. 500-490 B.C.
      Height: 22.2 cm.
      Diameter of base: 6.9 cm.

Side A: Herakles' combat with Kyknos
Side B: Athena and Ares

Herakles' combat with the Thessalian brigand Kyknos, a son of Ares, was one of his *parerga*, episodes that took place in the course of the hero's travels when he performed the twelve labors.

The story is not one of the more significant or colorful ones in Herakles' long career, but it is one of the best known to us in its details, thanks to a 480-line epic poem which survives, the *Shield of Herakles*. Attributed in antiquity to Hesiod, the poem is now thought to have been composed about a century after Hesiod's time, in the early sixth century. At about the same time the lyric poet Stesichoros wrote another version of the Kyknos story which is now lost. Together these poems inspired a full series of Attic vase-paintings, over one hundred of which are preserved, from the second quarter of the sixth century to the first quarter of the fifth. The scene occurs occasionally in sculpture as well, for example on one of the metopes of the Athenian Treasury at Delphi.

Painted depictions of the Kyknos story are always of one of two types: a single combat, in which only the two protagonists are shown; or a fuller version, in which Herakles is seconded by his patroness, Athena, and Kyknos by his father, Ares, with Zeus sometimes appearing in the middle, either to break up the fight or to show support for Herakles. The Virginia am-

phora is very unusual in showing the full version, but with the participants divided between the two sides of the vase.

On side A, Herakles leaps over the falling Kyknos. He wears his lion skin over a short *chiton*, his sword hanging from a baldric, and wields a spear. Kyknos' weapon is also a spear, and he wears a corselet and high crested Corinthian helmet. His shield device is two balls on a light ground. Several nonsense inscriptions appear in the field.

On side B, Ares and Athena stand back to back, their rear legs overlapping. Clearly we are meant to think of them as moving in the direction of their respective protégés on Side A. Ares wears hoplite armor, like his son, his shield device a winding serpent with gaping jaws. Athena wears her aegis over her extended left arm, like a shield, and a snake-like bracelet on her right wrist.

This vase is attributed to the Diosphos Painter, one of the latest black-figure artists, who began his career about 500 and may have continued well into the Early Classical period. He was primarily a painter of lekythoi, but the small neck-amphora with double-reeded handles and a special shape, sometimes called a doubleen, is also characteristic of his work.

Bibliography: Beazley, *Paralipomena* 250; *Ancient Art in the Virginia Museum* (Richmond 1973) 86. On Herakles and Kyknos: F. Vian, "Le combat d'Héraklès et de Kyknos d'après les documents figurés du VIe et du Ve siècle," *Revue des Etudes Anciennes* 47 (1945) 5-32.

Side A

Side B

25

Attic Black-Figure Amphora

Collection of the San Antonio Museum Association (75.59.15P)
Attributed to a painter of Group E [Bothmer]
Ca. 540-530 B.C.
Height: 40 cm.

Side A: Herakles rescuing Deianeira from the Centaur Nessos
Side B: Wheeling chariot

One day when Herakles was out with his wife Deianeira, they came to the River Evenos, in Aitolia, swollen with rain. The centaur Nessos offered to carry Deianeira across, but as Herakles watched from the bank, Nessos tried to take advantage of the woman in mid-stream. Herakles shot the centaur with an arrow made more lethal by having been dipped in the blood of the Hydra. But Nessos had his revenge, for with his dying words he persuaded Deianeira to save the blood from his wound and use it as a love potion, should Herakles ever wander in his affections. Years later, when Herakles brought home a concubine, the princess Iole, his distraught wife spread the potion on a shirt, a gift for Herakles, and thus unwittingly caused his agonizing death.

The death of Nessos was one of the earliest myth scenes to appear in Greek art, on a Proto-Attic amphora of the early seventh century, now in New York, and remained a popular subject in Attic black-figure. But the painted scenes seldom follow the canonical version of the story as recounted above, which is best known to us from Sophocles' *Trachiniae*. Instead, as on **side A** of this vase, Herakles' weapon is usually a sword, instead of bow and arrow, and there is no indication that the encounter takes places in or near a river. Herakles wears only a short *chiton* with a patterned hem; his scabbard hangs from a baldric across his chest. He puts his arm around his wife's shoulder, a protective gesture, as he advances toward the centaur.

Deianeira wears a belted *peplos* and a short shawl-like mantle over it. Nessos looks back as he runs off to the right, holding a stone in each hand. The centaurs live in the wild and regularly fight with whatever weapons are ready to hand - tree branches and rocks.

On side B, a four-horse chariot wheels sharply around, the rear horses animatedly kicking their forelegs high in the air. The chariot is driven by a bearded man in a pointed cap. He wears a short-sleeved *chiton* and over it a spotted animal hide, a frequent attribute of charioteers in black-figure. Beside him in the car stands a warrior in high crested Corinthian helmet, carrying a spear. Such lively chariot scenes are an especially common motif in later black-figure (compare [48]).

The San Antonio amphora has been assigned by Dietrich von Bothmer to Group E, a large but closely related group of black-figure painters of the third quarter of the sixth century. The E refers to the great master Exekias, for, in Beazley's words, this group is "the soil from which the art of Exekias rose, the tradition which he absorbs and transcends" (*The Development of Attic Black-Figure* [Berkeley 1951] 63). This vase exemplifies the one-piece or belly-amphora, with continuous curve from lip to foot. This type of amphora is generally earlier than that with offset neck, or neck-amphora, especially popular in later black figure (e.g. [48, 24, 2]).

Bibliography: Beazley, *Paralipomena* 56, 38 *bis*. Sale Catalog, Sotheby's, London 9 December, 1974, Lot 227, ill. On Herakles and Nessos: K. Fittschen, "Zur Herakles-Nessos-Sage," *Gymnasium* 77 (1970) 161-71. On the New York Nessos amphora: K. Schefold, *Frühgriechische Sagenbilder* (Munich 1964) 36 and pl. 23.

Side A

Side B

26

Attic Black-Figure Lekythos (White-Ground)

Collection of Gilbert M. Denman, Jr., San Antonio
Attributed to the Edinburgh Painter [Cahn]
Ca. 500 B.C.
 Height: 31.8 cm.
 Diameter: 11.5 cm.

Introduction of Herakles to Olympos

After Herakles' death, caused by the poisoned shirt of Nessos [25], and his immolation on a funeral pyre on Mount Oeta, he underwent an apotheosis, ascending to join the company of gods on Mount Olympos. The scene occurs often in Attic black-figure, starting in the second quarter of the sixth century, and continues, though less popular, throughout red-figure. The scene is usually referred to as the introduction, because Herakles is almost invariably accompanied by Athena, his protectress, who is sometimes seen presenting him to her father Zeus and the assembled gods and goddesses.

The apotheosis, or introduction, is generally shown in one of two ways: either Herakles is driven in a chariot by Athena; or, as here, they approach on foot. Generally speaking the introduction on foot is popular in earlier black-figure and is later replaced by the version with chariot, but the former type does recur, and the procession of vertical figures is certainly more appropriate for a narrow lekythos such as this example.

The scene is framed by two slender Doric columns which mark the entrance to Olympos. The group is led by Hermes, who gestures with upraised left hand, as if signalling to the unseen gods Herakles' arrival. Hermes wears winged boots and cap, *chlamys* over a short *chiton*, and carries his *kerykeion*. Next comes Athena, who looks back at Herakles, her raised hand also indicating that they have reached their destination. Her aegis, seen frontally, shows prominently the snaky fringe, and two snakes curl up over the goddess' shoulders. She wears a high-crested Attic helmet and carries a spear. Herakles wears only a short pleated *chiton* with short sleeves and carries his club in his right hand, a bow in his left. Behind him stands a bearded figure in a *chiton* and a tall pointed cap, holding two spears. This might be Iolaos, Herakles' frequent companion on most of his adventures [20], even though Iolaos could not, of course, accompany the hero to Olympos.

About 500 B.C. the Edinburgh Painter, to whom the Denman vase is attributed, introduced the technique of decorating larger cylindrical lekythoi with black figures on a white ground. It was only toward the middle of the fifth century that white-ground lekythoi became associated exclusively with the funerary cult [42-45]. This painter is also recognized by his distinctive pattern of five palmettes on the shoulder, the two outside ones facing the handle, and by his use of black paint for women's flesh, instead of the conventional white of standard black-figure.

Bibliography: H. Cahn, *Art of the Ancients* (New York 1968) 18. On the introduction of Herakles: P. Mingazzini, "Le rappresentazioni vascolari del mito dell' apoteosi di Herakles," *Atti della R. Accademia Nazionale dei Lincei*, Memorie della classe di scienze morali, storiche e fililogiche, ser. 6, 1 (1925) 413-490. On the Edinburgh Painter: D. C. Kurtz, *Athenian White Lekythoi* (Oxford 1975) 13-14.

27

Attic Black-Figure Amphora

Collection of the New Orleans Museum of Art, Gift of Alvin P. Howard
(16.38, formerly 2033)
Attributed to the Bucci Painter (Name Vase)
Ca. 530 B.C.

Height: 34.9 cm.
Diameter: 23.3 cm.

Side A: Herakles and Hermes
Side B: Horseman and companions

On side A, Herakles and Hermes stand on either side on a low rectangular altar. Herakles wears his lion skin over a short *chiton*. He customarily wears the animal's head pulled over his own, as here, like a hood, and the forepaws tied across his chest. A rear leg and the tail hang down low, below the hero's knees. He carries his club and wears a sword in its scabbard, hanging from a baldric. Hermes wears a striped *chlamys* draped over his left shoulder, winged shoes, and a cap, and carries the *kerykeion*. Hero and god gesture to each other with upraised left hand, probably a leave-taking, since Hermes moves off to the right while looking back. Perhaps the two have just performed a sacrifice.

The figures are framed by two slender Doric columns, reminiscent of those seen on Panathenaic amphoras. On the left hand column perches a cock, as on most Panathenaics, and on the right hand column an owl, which also occurs, though rarely (compare the Panathaic amphora in Austin [40], with owls on both columns). Nothing else about the vase suggests a Panathenaic context, and another vase probably by the same painter also has 'Panathenaic' columns; perhaps he simply borrowed them as a decorative element.

On side B, a horseman is mounted between four standing male companions. The horse is seen frontally, a relatively infrequent view, but with its head, as well as the rider's, in profile. The two figures at the right are both bearded and carry spears; those at left are beardless and unarmed, though one carries a staff. The scene probably shows a young warrior setting out. It may be mythological - a Trojan hero, perhaps - but need not be.

This New Orleans amphora is the name vase of the Bucci painter, so named by Dietrich von Bothmer for Donato Bucci of Civitavecchia, in whose collection it once was. At least fifteen vases have been attributed to him, and he is related in style both to the circle of the Antimenes Painter and to the red-figure Andokides Painter.

Bibliography: Beazley, *ABV*, 315,5; *Annali dell' Instituto di Corrispondenza Archaeologica* 1836, pl.F; E. Gerhard, *Etruskische und kampanische Vasenbilder* (Berlin 1843) pl. A, 19; D. von Bothmer, in *Studies Presented to David Moore Robinson* (St. Louis 1953) ii 135 and pl. 47. b-d; K. Schauenburg, in *Jahrbuch des Deutschen Archaeologischen Instituts* 94 (1979) 69, fig. 18.

Side A

Side B

28

Attic Black-Figure Eye-Cup

Collection of the Dallas Museum of Fine Arts, Gift of Mr. and Mrs. Cecil H. Green (1972.5)
Attributed to the Group of Walters 48.42
520-510 B.C.
> Height: 12.3 cm.
> Diameter (without handles): 31.7 cm.

Interior: Gorgoneion
Sides A and B: Herakles resting

On side A, Herakles reclines against a rock, holding a footless bowl without handles, a phiale, in his left hand. A soft cloak is casually draped over his left shoulder and arm. His traditional lion skin hangs magically behind him from the vase rim. His weapons, a sheathed sword with shoulder strap, bow, and arrow-filled quiver, also hang above him. The hero has been distracted from his contemplative mood by something behind him. While his powerful body remains in repose, his head snaps about in the direction of the disturbance and his right hand instinctively grasps his sword hilt. **On side B** of the cup, the scene is more tranquil. Herakles reclines once again on a rock, his weapons suspended above him. Clad in an elegant mantle, or *himation*, Herakles extends his high-handled wine cup, a kantharos, toward an obliging satyr who obediently fills his vessel from a wine skin. The lack of furniture and the rocky setting create an out-of-doors atmosphere to which the satyr adds a fitting touch. Scenes of Herakles reclining, whether after one of his labors or upon his arrival on Olympos, and attended by satyrs, appear on Attic black-figure vases during the late sixth century B.C.

Flanking each figured scene are large "female" eyes, almond-shaped and lacking extended tear ducts, with eyebrows. These were thought to provide an apotropaic service to the bearer. As John Boardman and others have noted, when the cup was tipped to the lips the fertile imagination of one's drinking companions saw a comical face with the cup handles serving as ears and the open, hollow foot as a mouth (see illustration). In the handle zones are painted vines and grape bunches which allude to the function of the cup as a container of wine. The cup interior holds a gorgoneion encircled by a net pattern.

The Dallas vase can be placed with a series of type A cups known as the Group of Walters 48.42 from its name piece in Baltimore. The vase shape, feminine eyes, grape vines in the handle zones, alternating outline and silhouette rays from the foot, and the style of the gorgoneion are all characteristics of vases in this group. The draftsmanship of the Dallas cup, however, is far superior to most examples in the group and incorporates a number of elements adopted from contemporary Attic red-figure painting, such as the attempt at forshortening of Herakles' left foot on side A and the oblique angle of his abdominal muscles, to create the impression of his twisting motion. The undulating lines of his cloak on side A are a welcome change from the stiff banded folds of earlier black-figure, while the sweeping curves of Herakles' *himation* on side B recall those of the reclining Herakles' dress on the well known bilingual amphora in Munich by the Andokides Painter (Beazley, *ARV²* 4,9), himself a contemporary red-figure artist.

KARL KILINSKI II

Bibliography: Unpublished. On the Group of Walters 48.42: Beazley, *ABV* 205-207 and *Paralipomena* 94-97. On Herakles resting with satyrs: Brommer *Vasenlisten*³ 191-192.

Side A

Side B

Interior

Heroes

Apart from Herakles, all Greek heroes were most closely associated with their native city or region and tended to receive cult worship only there. Yet at the same time they were all panhellenic, in the sense that poets from all parts of Greece celebrated their deeds in verse, and vase-painters in Athens, Corinth, and elsewhere drew on the rich resources of heroic legend for their subjects. Because the survival of ancient literature is so capricious, many heroic myths are better known to us from the pictorial than from the written tradition. For example, although the heroes who fought at Troy are familiar to us from the two Homeric poems, *Iliad* and *Odyssey*, many of their deeds before and during the war were told in other epic poems that do not survive. But vase-paintings fill in our knowledge of these events, such as the Judgment of Paris [37], the death of Achilles [35], the sack of Troy, and Menelaos' recovery of Helen [37]. The artists of the sixth and fifth centuries had full access to this so-called Epic Cycle of poems about Troy, in addition to knowing all the stories by heart, and, after Herakles, these were the prime source of material for mythological scenes.

Since Theseus was thought of as the Athenian hero *par excellence*, we expect him to be a favorite of Attic artists, and in some periods this is true, though, surprisingly, not with the same consistency as Herakles. As one of the legendary kings of Attica, Theseus shared in the general awakening of Athenian interest in the city's early history after the victory over the Persians in 480. The bringing of his bones to Athens and the building of a sanctuary in his honor, in the 460's, further elevated his status. Before that, in the Archaic period, Theseus had been known for only one celebrated deed, the slaying of the Minotaur on Crete, and his appearances in Attic black-figure are, with few exceptions, limited to this role. The turning point apparently came in 510, with the overthrow of the Peisistratid tyranny and the establishment of a democracy under Kleisthenes. Theseus was invoked as the hero of the new Athens, and the reorganization of the Attic demes by Kleisthenes into ten tribes named for Eponymous Heroes [32] was likened to Theseus' supposed unification of Attica. To match the labors of Herakles, Theseus was given a set of heroic deeds, performed as a youth along the road from Troizen to Athens, where he was recognized by his father, King Aigeus, as the son sired many years before on the Troizenian princess Aithra. One more deed, the capture of the Bull of Marathon [30], confirmed his royal descent.

The capture of a great bull was not the only adventure shared by both Herakles and Theseus. At different times each encountered the Amazons, that fierce race of women warriors who lived in a remote area near the Black Sea. Herakles travelled to the land of the Amazons to obtain the girdle of their queen, Hippolyte, by dint of a great battle which is often depicted in Attic black-figure. Theseus' Amazonomachy was on home ground, when the Amazons stormed the Acropolis and he and his friend Perithoos led the defense [31]. Both battles came to be seen in the Classical period as prototypes for Greek victory over non-Greek barbarians (i.e. Persians), hence their enormous popularity in Classical art, both painting and sculpture. Even in quieter moments Amazons continued to fascinate Greek artists [33, 34], both for their exoticism and for their striking contrast to the docile submissiveness of everyday Athenian women.

Many other heroes were the subjects of rich bodies of myth: Jason and the voyage of the Argonauts; the Seven Against Thebes; Bellerophon, who slew the Chimaira; and Perseus, who slew the Gorgon [38], to name only a few. All of these were represented by Greek vase-painters, though none as exhaustively as the heroes of Troy, Herakles, and Theseus. For reasons we do not fully understand, some myths which were of little interest to Greek artists appealed to fourth-century vase-painters in South Italy, to the Etruscans, or to the Romans centuries later.

29

Attic Black-Figure Neck-Amphora

Collection of the Duke University Museum of Art, Durham (1974.6)
Leagros Group [D. K. Stanley]
Late sixth century B.C.
Height: 29.8 cm.
Diameter: 19 cm.

Side A: Peleus wrestling Thetis
Side B: Theseus slaying the Minotaur

This typical late black-figure amphora, with its echinus mouth, triple handles and torus foot, portrays two mythological scenes, both extremely popular in Attic vase painting. While not specifically related, the scenes share a similar compositional scheme: a pair of combatants in the center flanked by two females.

Side A shows a half-draped young man with long hair and sword at his waist embracing a woman. She wears a long *chiton* and is gesticulating wildly, as are her two companions who flee from the scene. The one at the right holds a long vine, and hence might be taken to be a maenad. However, such tendrils constitute background filler on many late black-figure vases, and so are not relevant to an interpretation of the scene. The manner in which the man embraces the woman, a body hold, shows that they are wrestling, and so could be none other than Peleus and his future bride, the sea nymph Thetis. The match is popular is Attic vase-painting not only for its intrinsic dramatic appeal, but also because from their union came the great hero Achilles.

Side B, distinguished from side A by the up-and-down palmettes on the neck in place of the palmette-lotus chain, shows a less friendly combat, a duel to the death. The youth in the short *chiton* is Theseus and his bull-headed opponent is the Minotaur. The monster has fallen to his knee and attempts to defend himself with the white rock clutched in his left hand. Theseus, however, has a firm grasp on the Minotaur's left forearm and has plunged his sword into the monster's chest. Red blood spurts from the wound. The pair are flanked by two draped women; the one behind the hero encouraging him is perhaps Ariadne, the other an anonymous Athenian maiden, part of the tribute to King Minos. In addition to their compositional similarities, the two sides of this vase share an amorous intent: young Greek heroes fighting for their future brides.

JENIFER NEILS

Bibliography: Sale Catalog, Christie's, London, 10 July, 1974, lot 112, p. 37 pl. 34. On the wrestling match of Peleus and Thetis: Brommer, *Vasenlisten*³, 321-329. On Theseus and the Minotaur: Brommer, *Vasenlisten*³, 226-243.

Side A

Side B

30

Attic Red-Figure Bell-Krater

Collection of Mr. and Mrs. Edward L. Diefenthal, Metairie, Louisiana
Manner of the Dinos Painter [Bothmer]
Ca. 425 B.C.

Height: 29 cm.
Diameter: 31.4 cm.

Side A: Theseus and the Marathonian Bull
Side B: Three Draped Youths

Of the deeds of the hero Theseus, the most popular in Attic vase-painting after the Minotauroctony is the capture of the wild bull ravaging the plain of Marathon. It appears first on the early cups which depict the youthful deeds of the hero in cyclical fashion, ca. 520-510 B.C., and endures longer than any other new exploit, undergoing various transformations. The earliest depictions, notably those on the late Archaic cycle cups, show Theseus in the process of hobbling the bull. In the early Classical period the moment changes, and we find the hero, club in hand, driving the restive beast to Athens. By ca. 450 B.C., a third participant has been added to the scene, a woman running before the bull and holding libation vessels. In no instance is she labeled and there is some controversy over her identification.

The Diefenthal krater clearly belongs to this third group, both in date and iconography. Theseus, nude except for a *pilos* or traveling cap, a cloak over his left arm, and a baldric across his chest, is shown restraining the lunging bull by means of a club and a rope attached to the animal's horns. Ahead of the bull runs a woman wearing a belted *peplos*, her hair tied up in a beaded fillet. As she moves to the right, she looks back at Theseus, holding forth a phiale in her outstretched right hand. In her left she carries a trefoil-lipped oinochoe viewed from the top. It has been argued by many that this woman is either a local nymph running away in fright, or the female personification of the locale, Marathon. However, just as Theseus is recognizable by his traveling attire and club, so this woman should be identified by her attributes. We know from mythological sources that the sorceress Medea attempted to poison the hero upon his arrival in Athens before he was recognized by his father Aigeus. In the extant accounts the timing of her attempt varies, either before or after the bull episode. But, whenever it took place, it seems reasonable to regard this woman with her offering vessels, who appears to be fleeing in fear of the consequences of her foiled attempt on the hero's life, as Medea. This identification is supported by other depictions of the scene which show a woman in the same pose with the same attributes, but in oriental costume (i.e., a sleeved outfit), an indisputable allusion to Medea's non-Greek origins. Therefore, this vase-painting of Theseus depicts not one youthful agon, but two: his conquest over the brute forces of nature exemplified by the bull, and his victory over the forces of evil personified by Medea.

The painting on the reverse is non-mythological and purely conventional. Three youths, enveloped in their mantles, stand conversing. The locale is the palaestra, as indicated by the objects hanging in the field: an aryballos or ointment jar hanging between the first and second youths; a strigil between the second and third.

The bell krater is a popular shape in the Classical period, and this scheme of decoration with a mythological scene on the front and secondary filler on the back is very common. The vase is related to others done in the manner of the Dinos Painter, an artist who specialized in larger pots, especially kraters.

JENIFER NEILS

Bibliography: Unpublished. On Theseus and the Marathonian bull: Brommer, *Vasenlisten*³ 252-257; B.B. Shefton, "Medea at Marathon," *American Journal of Archaeology* 60 (1956) 159-163, pls. 60-61. On the Dinos Painter and his followers: Beazley, *ARV*² 1151-1158.

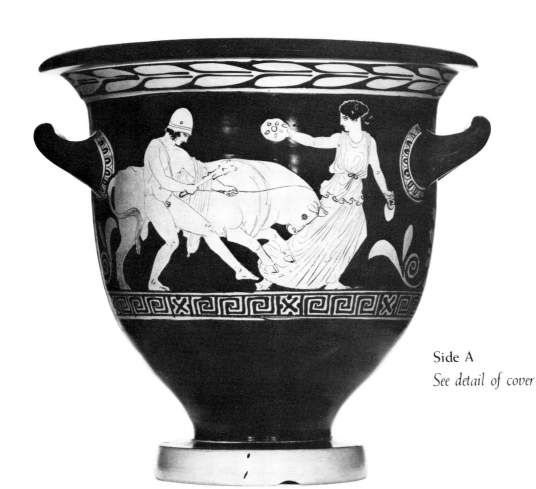

Side A
See detail of cover

Side B

31

Attic Red-Figure Neck Amphora

Collection of The University Museums, University of Mississippi Phase I Cultural
    Center (1977.3.97)
Attributed to the Group of Polygnotos
440-430 B.C.
    Height: 42.2 cm.
    Diameter: 24.1 cm.

Side A: Theseus, Peirithoos and Amazon
Side B: Three youths in mantles

The Amazon **on side A** holds her bow in the left hand and retreats to the right, turning to strike with her battle-ax at Theseus, whose spear has already penetrated her side. Only the distinctive ax marks her as an Amazon; instead of the usual patterned tights she wears a Greek *peplos*. Behind Theseus his friend Peirithoos prepares to throw a stone. The figures are not named, but each is labeled "beautiful" — kalos, kalos, kale. This is one of six vases, all from the same circle of painters and all with the same three-figure composition, differing slightly in details of weaponry and costume, which probably go back to a common original. On one of the other vases the central figure is labeled "Theseus," and the identification should hold good for all six. Theseus is heroically nude except for his helmet; the painter has given Peirithoos a shaggy pilos and an animal-skin cloak, perhaps in reference to his rustic Thessalian homeland.

The combats of Achilles and Herakles against Amazons appear in vase painting after about 550 B.C., but Theseus' Amazonomachies begin in the last quarter of the century, when the Athenians were attempting to raise their national hero to equal status with Herakles. An epic poem, the *Theseis* was perhaps composed about 525, and illustrations of episodes from the epic appear soon afterward. The theme of Theseus' defeat of an Amazon army that invaded Attica to avenge his abduction of their queen became especially popular after the Athenian repulse of the Persian invasions of Attica in 490 and 480 B.C. Greek artists seldom represented historical events directly, preferring to look to the legendary past for a parallel event; thus for artists working in Athens, the Amazon invasion became a visual metaphor for the Persian ones, and Amazonomachies were chosen as the theme for decorating several public buildings. The common ancestor for the examples of this three-figure composition could be either a wall painting or another vase painting. Two large-scale Amazonomachies of Theseus were painted in Athenian buildings in the generation after the Persian Wars, one by Mikon and one by Polygnotos of Thasos (not the vase painter of the same name). No detailed description of either painting survives, but 5th-century vase painters are believed to have copied some of Polygnotos' innovations: many-figured compositions, the placement of figures at different levels rather than on a common ground line, and the use of trees and other landscape features. The Theseus-Amazon pair from this vase also occur on at least four other vases, as part of many-figured Amazonomachies with Polygnotan characteristics. Variations on the Peirithoos figure also occur in these pictures, and it is likely that this group was derived from a larger vase-painting that in turn was derived from a wall painting.

LUCY TURNBULL

Bibliography: D.M. Robinson, "Unpublished Greek Vases in the Robinson Collection," *American Journal of Archaeology* 60 (1956) 1-25, pl. 16, 71-2. Beazley, *ARV²* 1058. D. von Bothmer, *Amazons in Greek Art* (Oxford 1957) 185-191; pl. 81, 4. For Theseus' significance in Attic art and politics: A. Ward, *The Quest for Theseus* (New York 1970); for relationships between wall painting and vase painting: E. Simon, "Polygnotan Painting and the Niobid Painter," *American Journal of Archaeology* 67 (1963) 43-62.

Side A

Side B

32

Attic Red-Figure Ram's Head Rhyton

Collection of the Virginia Museum of Fine Arts, Richmond, The Williams
    Fund, (79.100)
Signed by Charinos as potter; attributed to the Triptolemos Painter [Ohly-Dumm]
480-470 B.C.

> Height (restored): 21.95 cm.
> Height of figured frieze: 6.35 cm.
> Diameter of cup: 11.48 cm.

Symposium of Attic Kings

Five symposiasts recline around the cup attached to the top of this magnificent molded ram's head. The four drinkers (1, 2, 4, 5) rest on striped pillows, their legs to the left enveloped in their mantles, upper bodies frontal and heads in profile. The middle man (3) is also semi-reclining, but has less use for his pillow as he sits up to play his lyre; his left foot protrudes from the drapery around his legs. Costume, attributes and age also vary among the symposiasts. (1) is middle-aged, bearded, and his long black hair is rolled up around a fillet. Under his mantle he wears a sleeveless *chiton*, and he is distinguished from the other guests by having two cups: a black-glazed kantharos resting in his left hand, and a kylix with offset lip in his up-raised right hand. He holds one handle with his index finger and is clearly about to toss the dregs in the popular Greek drinking game known as *kottabos*. Before aiming he looks back at his nearest companion (2), an elderly white-haired gentleman, who is similarly dressed and also holding a kantharos in his left hand. These two are closely linked not only by position, but by gesture as well; the older man, right hand raised, hails the younger. The third figure (3), a mature, dark-haired man, lacks a *chiton* under his mantle, and, more significantly, a drinking cup. He appears to be tuning his *barbiton* or lyre, and remains a bit aloof from the assembled company. The only youth on the vase (4) takes the fourth position; beardless, he nonetheless has soft, downy sideburns on his cheeks, and wears his hair in the "severe" style, i.e., rolled up over a fillet with tight curls encircling the face. He also lacks a *chiton*, but holds a black kantharos in his right hand. Like (1) he turns to look at the figure directly behind, an older, white-haired man (5). Dressed like the other elderly smyposiast (2), this one is distinguished by his odd mug-like drinking cup and by his gesture: he strokes his beard as he stares at the comely youth before him. The festive setting is indicated not only by the presence of pillows and drinking vessels, but by the musical instruments hanging on the wall behind, two lyres and a *cithara* decorated with apotropaic eyes.

While banqueting scenes and drinking parties are commonplace in Attic vase-painting, especially in the Late Archaic period, this particular symposium is unique among them. First, one is struck by the presence of kantharoi among the drinking vessels. This cup with high-swung double handles is the specific attribute of none other that the god of wine himself, Dionysos (see [12]). It is almost never used by mortals, and only occasionally by heroes, usually Herakles at the end of his labors when he assumes semi-divine status. But even more useful in distinguishing these figures as heroes of legend are the inscriptions above their heads. (1) is labeled KEKROPS, an early, legendary king of Athens, and (4) is labeled THESEUS, the Attic hero *par excellence*, best known for his victory over the Cretan Minotaur, after which,

Bibliography: J. Neils, *The Youthful Deeds of Theseus: Iconography and Iconology*, Ph.D. diss., Princeton University (Princeton 1980) 221, 224-225, no. 37, ill. 151. R. Guy, "A Ram's Head Rhyton Signed by Charinos," *Arts in Virginia* 21 (1981) 2-15. For Attic kings and eponymous heroes: F. Brommer, "Attische Könige," *Charites. Studien zur Altertumswissenschaft* [Festschrift Ernst Langlotz] (Bonn 1957) 152-164, pls. 21-22; U. Kron, *Die zehn attischen Phylenheroen* (Berlin 1976); E. B. Harrison, "The Iconography of the Eponymous Heroes on the Parthenon and in the Agora," *Greek Numismatics and Archaeology: Essays in Honor of Margaret Thompson* (Wetteren, 1979) 71-85. On the Triptolemos Painter: Beazley, *ARV²* 360-367. On Charinos: Beazley, *ARV²* 1531-1532. On rhyta: H. Hoffmann, *Attic Red-Figured Rhyta* (Mainz, 1962).

and following his father Aegeus' untimely death, he also became king of Athens. These names suggest that we are dealing here with a royal gathering of different generations. Who might the others be? Unfortunately, the inscribed names are not completely preserved. (3) is partially labeled -UPOP-, but the letters cannot be restored to correspond to the name of any Attic king or hero, unless it proved to be a misspelling of the eponymous tribal hero Hippothoön. More likely, it is simply part of the name of a professional bard called upon to entertain at this illustrious symposium. Finally, the remainder of a name ending in the letters -ON is attached to the last figure (5). Given the fact that he is depicted as two generations removed from Theseus, he might well be identified as Pandion, the hero's grandfather and another king of Athens. That leaves the second symposiast (2) yet to be identified. Possibilities among Attic kings include: Erectheus, the father of Kekrops; Erichthonios, who is often confused with the former as both were raised by Athena (see [4]); or Aigeus, the father of Theseus. The age of the man argues for one of the first two; the space limitations above his head perhaps for the third. However, if the same rules regarding age relationships and juxtaposition of figures operate here as on the other side, then the most likely identification of the two is father and son. Also, Erectheus, as the prime Athenian ancestor, should not be missing from this royal assembly.

It remains to explain why these Attic kings should be depicted together at all. It has been suggested, because of the date of the vase, that they are celebrating the recent victory of the Greeks over the Persians. However, given the prominence of the youngest hero on the cup, and the fact that Greek vase-painting is more likely to deal with mythological than historical events, it is perhaps more reasonable to assume that the Attic kings have assembled to accept Theseus into their ranks, in which case the bard may well be singing the hero's great feats either in Crete or on the Isthmian Road. While there is no other depiction of Theseus directly comparable to that on the Richmond rhyton, it is at precisely this time (ca. 480-460 B.C.) that interest in the youth of the hero reaches its apogee among artists as well as poets. Not only are there quantitatively more vase-painting from this period, but the range of subjects is considerably expanded; in particular, one finds a new concern in establishing the hero's Athenian connections. All of this is not surprising when one recalls that ca. 470 B.C. the Athenian naval commander Kimon brought the bones of the hero back to the city and laid them in the Theseion, a shrine dedicated to the hero. Such a magnificent piece of both modeling and painting as this ram's head rhyton may well have served as a dedication in such a shrine.

The painting on the cup is attributed to the Triptolemos Painter, a cup-painter of the Late Archaic period, who in his early phase owes much to Douris. Later, and as this vase demonstrates, he is closer to the Brygos Painter, who also painted symposia on the cups of rhyta. An anonymous, presumably mortal symposium by the Triptolemos Painter appears on the exterior of a cup in Berlin (Staatliche Museen 2298: Beazley, *ARV*² 364, 52), and provides a close parallel for the Richmond vase.

The rhyton is signed by the potter Charinos, previously known exclusively as the maker of human-head kantharoi and oinochoai, on the majority of which his name is incised on the handle. Here the potter's signature is painted along the juncture of the two halves of the ram's face. Both the modeling and painting of the ram's head are very expressive and naturalistic, in contrast to the ornamental palmettes on the back. The foot is restored.

JENIFER NEILS

33

Attic White-Ground Alabastron

Collection of the Virginia Museum of Fine Arts, Richmond, The Williams
  Fund (78.145)
Attributed to the Syriskos Painter [Cahn]
470-460 B.C.
    Height: 15.2 cm.
    Diameter: 5.4 cm.

Side A: Amazon
Side B: Palm tree and stool

On side A, an Amazon moves to the right, but turns to look back. She is dressed in special oriental garb: a cuirass over a short *chiton* (only the hem of which is shown, in dilute glaze) over black *anaxyrides* (trousered and sleeved outfit) decorated with red dots and stripes, with a long black *chlamys* or cloak worn shawl-like over both arms. The cuirass is decorated with dotted saltires on the shoulder flaps and an abbreviated meander at the neck and waist. The female warrior is armed with a *gorytos* or quiver at her waist, a battle axe in her right hand, and a *pelta* or lunette shield in her left. **Side B** is considerably plainer, showing only a palm tree with twisted trunk, and a simple stool or *diphros*.

The white-ground alabastron, a perfume vase which imitates its alabaster prototype both in shape and color, often bears exotic subject matter. Those with Amazons, such as the Richmond example, are closely related stylistically and iconographically to Beazley's "Group of the Negro Alabastra," where Negro warriors, similarly attired and posed, replace their female counterparts. These foreign types have in common the fact that they both came to the aid of Troy after the death of Hector, the Negroes under the Ethiopian prince Memnon, and the Amazons following their queen, Penthesilea. Although distinct racially and geographically, these foreigners share a common costume and armament — both invented by the Attic vase-painters to connote a "barbarian" or non-Greek. Likewise, the palm tree on the reverse indicates a distant, alien land.

This vase is attributed to the Syriskos Painter, an important red-figure artist of the transitional period between late Archaic and early Classic, whose workshop produced the majority of the Negro alabastra. Similar, but slightly earlier "Amazon alabastra" by his hand are in the British Museum (B673) and in the Badisches Landesmuseum, Carlsruhe (69/34). The Richmond Amazon, however, is distinguished from her sisters by her more fashionable attire: black slippers, hoop earring, and curly hair tied up in back. Both the classical features of this Amazon and the vase's place at the end of the development of the type indicate a date in the second quarter of the fifth century B.C.

JENIFER NEILS

Bibliography: Herbert A. Cahn, *Classical Antiquity*, sale cat. (Zürich: André Emmerich Gallery Inc., 1976) no. 18; Jenifer Neils, "The Group of the Negro Alabastra: A Study in Motif Transferal," *Antike Kunst* 23 (1980) 20, no. 62, pl. 7, 5-7. For Amazons on white-ground alabastra: Neils, *op. cit.*, pp. 18-20, nos. 48-62; Dietrich von Bothmer, *Amazons in Greek Art* (Oxford 1957) 152, nos. 67-77. On the Syriskos Painter and his workshop: Beazley, *ARV²* 256-270.

Side A   Side B

34

Attic Red-Figure Pelike

Collection of the University of Arkansas Museum, Fayetteville (57-24-2)
Attributed to the Biscoe Painter
Ca. 450-440 B. C.

> Height: 24.5 cm.
> Diameter: 19 cm.

Side A: Two Amazons mounted on horseback
Side B: Three youths

On side A, two armed warriors ride to the right. Each wears a leather cuirass over a short linen *chiton* and an Attic helmet with a crest which disappears into the upper border. They wear shoes, but no greaves (shinguards). Each carries two spears. The warriors might easily be taken for young, beardless Athenian hoplites, but a comparison with similar scenes in Attic red-figure of this period, some of which label the figures, shows that they are in fact Amazons. In earlier vase-painting, Amazons are usually easily distinguished from the Greek male hoplites with whom they fight, either by added white paint for female flesh (in black-figure) or by their exotic dress and armor which recall Thracians or Scythians. But by the mid-fifth century, their armor is often indistinguishable from that of Greek hoplites, and they are increasingly shown in quiet scenes, like this one, rather than in combat.

The scene on this pelike may be one of many in this period that reflect the influence of two famous but now lost Athenian wall paintings of the Battle of Greeks and Amazons. One was in the Stoa Poikile, on the north side of the Agora, the other in the Theseion, whose location is not known but may have been on the lower north slope of the Acropolis. Both paintings were done about 460, the former by the great painter Mikon, the latter perhaps by the same artist. One source specifically mentions that Mikon painted Amazons on horseback (Aristophanes, *Lysistrata* 678-79).

Side B shows three beardless youths engaged in conversation. All wear similar mantles, and the one at left carries a staff. The draughtsmanship here is startlingly careless in comparison with the fine style of Side A.

The painter, who is named for a pelike now in Los Angeles (Beazley, *ARV²* 1063, top, 2), was placed by Beazley "on the outskirts of the Polygnotan Group," that is, somewhat distantly related to one of the leading painters of larger pots in the mid-fifth century, Polygnotos. Of the Amazons on this vase, however, Beazley wrote that the scene is a very close imitation of the style of Polygnotos himself. Polygnotos in turn came out of the school of the Niobid Painter, and both artists were profoundly influenced by innovations in monumental painting of the Early Classical period. Here is, then, one more reason to suspect that these Amazons find their ultimate inspiration in a lost masterpiece of wall painting.

Bibliography: Beazley, *ARV²* 1063, top, 1; D. von Bothmer, *Amazons in Greek Art* (Oxford 1957) 199, no. 140 and pl. 83,4; Q. Maule, "Greek Vases in Arkansas," *American Journal of Archaeology* 75 (1971) 89-91 and pl. 24, fig. 13-14. On Amazons, and Amazonomachies in monumental painting: Bothmer, *op. cit.*, especially 163; 200.

Side A

Side B

35

Attic Black-Figure Neck Amphora

Collection of the North Carolina Museum of Art, Raleigh, (74.1.6)
Leagros Group
Ca. 500 B.C.
> Height: 34.3 cm.
> Diameter: 21.9 cm.

Side A: Ajax with the body of Achilles
Side B: Fight

When Achilles was slain at Troy by Paris' arrow, it was Ajax who rescued the body and carried it from the battlefield. Ironically, the rescued armor would later prove to be the brave Ajax' undoing, when it was awarded to Odysseus instead of to him. Ajax carrying Achilles' corpse first appears in Attica on the François Vase of about 570, where the figures are labelled. In several dozen later instances, such as the North Carolina example, the motif of a warrior carrying the body of a dead comrade is usually assumed to refer to the same heroic pair, even without inscriptions to assure their identity.

On side A, Ajax walks slowly but in long strides under his great burden, moving toward the left, as is usual in such scenes. He wears a short belted *chiton*, greaves, scabbard suspended at the waist, and a low crested Corinthian helmet. He carries two spears in his right hand and his shield on his left arm; the device is a frontal lion or panther head. Achilles wears the same outfit, except that his helmet has a tall crest and his shield device is a frontal satyr's head. At the left a woman runs off, looking back, one hand raised in fright. She may be identified as Thetis, Achilles' mother. She wears a sleeveless *chiton* and *himation*, and a fillet in her hair.

On side B, two warriors engage in combat, as a third moves in from the right to support his falling comrade. All three are fully armed in greaves, short pleated *chiton*, corselet, and high crested Corinthian helmet. The falling central warrior has as his shield device a tripod; his companion, three balls. Their opponent's shield is seen from the inside, his left arm through the *porpax*, or strap. This is a type of shield known as Boeotian, oval with two half-moon shaped cutouts. The other two are the more standard round hoplite shields. All fight with spears and have sheathed swords hanging from baldrics across their chests. One would like to connect this scene with the Trojan subject on the other side, but in the absence of inscriptions or other specific information the figures cannot be identified.

Bibliography: *Bulletin, North Carolina Museum of Art* 13, 1-2 (1976) no. 103; p. 39 (ill.); *ibid.* 13, 3 (1976) 32-33 (ill.); *Gazette de Beaux-Arts*, Paris (March, 1976) no. 1286; p. 32, ill. 32. On Ajax with the body of Achilles: S. Woodford and M. Loudon, "Two Trojan Themes," *American Journal of Archaeology* 84 (1980) 25-40. (This vase should be added to Appendix I, p. 36, Group C).

Side A

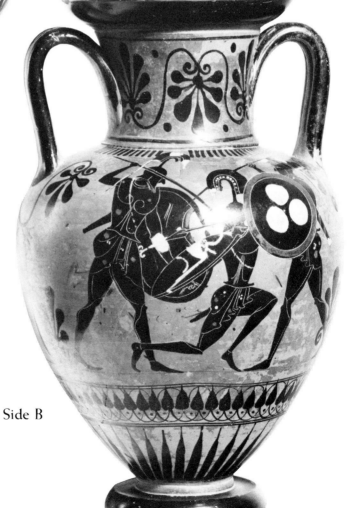

Side B

93

36

Attic Red-Figure Pelike

Collection of The University Museums, University of Mississippi Phase I Cultural
   Center (1977. 3. 99)
Attributed to the Calliope Painter
430-420 B. C.
   Height: 19.1 cm.
   Diameter: 16.1 cm.

Side A: Hector (?) arming
Side B: Priam (?)

A young man stands pulling off his cloak with his right hand while with the left he takes the spear and helmet the woman holds for him. She carries his shield, which bears a lion as its device, and gazes at him over its rim. On the reverse, an older man stands holding a scepter and looking intently before him. He must belong with the two figures on side A, in the traditional grouping of a departing warrior between his parents. This was one of the longest-lived themes in Greek vase-painting, as well as in Greek life. War was endemic in the Greek world, with cities constantly quarreling among themselves, and every male citizen could expect to be in battle many times in the course of his life. This pelike was painted in the early years of the Peloponnesian War, when scenes like this one were being enacted frequently in Athenian homes. No names are given here; the young man looks like a contemporary Athenian whose wife or mother is helping him with his weapons and shield, all of which are conventional 5th-century heavy infantry equipment. If this were meant to be a contemporary scene, however, we would expect to see more armor; a breastplate certainly, if not also a pair of greaves. A young man who goes out to battle wearing only a helmet and a sword belt is more likely to be a legendary hero, at least in vase-painting. The bearded man on side B gives another clue to the warrior's identity: from his wreath and scepter, he must be a king, and the hero leaving home is his son. In all probability he is Priam, and the young man Hector, while the woman may be his mother or his wife Andromache.

The painter has set his figures well apart, and has made the helmet the focal point of the picture by setting it at the crossing point of the vertical line of the spear and the diagonal lines of the two arms. These diagonals are extended and made more emphatic by the line of the cloak which Hector pulls off with his right hand and by the body of the lion on the shield. The helmet is held almost at eye level; are the figures looking at it or at each other? Perhaps we have here an echo of the touching scene in the *Iliad* (6. 369-502) of Hector's farewell to his wife Andromache, who begs him not to go back to the battle, and to their baby son, who takes fright and begins to cry at the sight of his father's helmet, with its crest "nodding terribly, as he thought." The mood here is quiet and restrained, as in much of the art of the period, but there is something of poignancy in the two faces regarding each other over the crest of the helmet.

LUCY TURNBULL

Bibliography: Beazley, *ARV*² 1262, 60.

Side A

Side B

95

37

Attic Black-Figure Neck Amphora

Collection of the Virginia Museum of Fine Arts, Richmond, The Williams
  Fund (57.9)
Attributed to the Antimenes Painter
Ca. 520-510 B.C.
  Height: 34.4 cm.

Side A: Judgment of Paris
Side B: Recovery of Helen

Both scenes are part of the Trojan cycle, and there is a narrative link between the two in the person of Helen. It was Paris' theft of Helen, the wife of King Menelaos of Sparta, that precipitated the Trojan War, and it was Aphrodite who promised Helen to Paris at the Judgment. Ten years later, the War finally having ended with the Greek sack of Troy, Menelaos recovers his wayward queen, to take her home to Sparta.

The Judgment of Paris (**side A**) was a favorite subject in Greek art from the seventh century down to the end of the Classical period. In later black-figure, as on this vase, Paris himself is often not shown, and the scene must be understood as the three goddesses making their way to Mount Ida, conducted there by Hermes. Of the three, Athena is usually most easily recognized, by her helmet, and is most often in the middle. In black-figure it is sometimes difficult to distinguish Hera and Aphrodite. The standard order is for Hera to lead the group, with Aphrodite bringing up the rear; that is probably the case here, since the staff carried by the front figure could be interpreted as Hera's sceptre. Otherwise the two goddesses look remarkably similar and even make the same gesture, sniffing a flower. Hermes wears traditional travelling attire: winged boot, short *chiton* and *chlamys*, and he holds the *kerykeion*.

The Recovery of Helen (**side B**) also has a long pedigree in Greek art, going back to the seventh century, and this Richmond vase shows the most canonical version of the myth as represented in Attic black-figure. Menelaos rather brusquely grasps his wife's hand, threatening her with his sword and glaring back at her as he starts to walk off to the right. Helen hesitates, standing stiffly, her mantle pulled down over her head like a veil. As if Menelaos' drawn sword were not persuasive enough, a second Greek sword behind Helen encourages her to move along. This may belong to Odysseus, who accompanied Menelaos during the last night at Troy. Both warriors are dressed alike in greaves, short pleated *chiton*, corselet, and Corinthian helmet, Menelaos' with a tall crest, Odysseus' with a low one. Two draped figures, apparently male, overlapping the handle palmettes, symmetrically frame the scene, but seem to be meant only as filler, rather than as integral parts of the narrative.

The vase is attributed to the Antimenes Painter, one of the major black-figure artists of the first generation after the invention of red-figure, who is fond of Trojan subjects and painted several other versions of each of these scenes.

Bibliography: Beazley, *ABV* 271,78 and 691,78*bis; Paralipomena* 118,78; E. Gerhard, *Auserlesene griechische Vasenbilder* (Berlin 1840-58) pl. 72; *Ancient Art in the Virginia Museum* (Richmond 1973) 96-97. On the Judgment of Paris: Chr. Clairmont, *Das Parisurteil in der antiken Kunst* (Zurich 1951); I. Raab, *Zu den Darstellungen des Parisurteils in der Kunst* (Frankfurt 1972). On the Recovery of Helen: L. B. Ghali-Kahil, *Les enlèvements et le retour d'Hélène* (Paris 1955).

Side A

Side B

38

Attic Red-Figure Hydria

Collection of the Virginia Museum of Fine Arts, Richmond, The Williams
   Fund (62.1.1)
Attributed to the Nausicaa Painter
Ca. 450 B.C.
   Height: 45.5 cm.

Perseus beheading Medusa

The myth of Perseus beheading the Gorgon Medusa was especially popular in Proto-Attic and early Attic black-figure, a century and more before the period of this vase. After that the scene recurs only sporadically, and this version is one of the latest known. In Archaic art, the moment in the story most often depicted is the chase after the beheading, when Perseus flees with the severed head, pursued by Medusa's sisters. In only a few red-figure scenes of the mid-fifth century, including this one, do we see the hero sneaking up on his victim as she sleeps.

Medusa is very much the center of attention in the composition, the focus of all eyes. She sleeps peacefully against the trunk of a tree, her left wing apparently hidden by the rising ground. The frontal face is a relatively rare occurrence in Attic vase-painting and is generally restricted to a few specific purposes, including the depiction of sleeping figures. Medusa wears a short pleated *chiton* with short sleeves. In the course of the fifth century she gradually loses the monstrous features that had characterized her since her first appearances in Greek art in the seventh century. Eventually she will emerge as a beautiful young woman, as on a famous pelike in New York (Beazley, *ARV²* 1032,55). On the Richmond vase the transformation is not complete, as indicated by the broad nose and huge gaping mouth, with protruding tongue.

Perseus approaches stealthily from the right, holding in his left hand the *kibisis*, or leather pouch in which he will carry the head, and in his right a sickle (*harpe*). Behind him stands his guide, Hermes, identified by his traveller's hat (*petasos*) and *kerykeion*. Perseus seems unaware of the power of Medusa's gaze to turn men to stone, for he does not, as on most vases, avert his eyes.

Athena stands opposite Perseus and reaches out her right hand, as if cautioning the hero against making noise and awakening the Gorgon. She wears a large Corinthian helmet and carries a spear. Her aegis, which will later carry the Gorgon's head as an apotropaic device, is not seen. Behind Athena sits a stately bearded figure, wearing a fillet in his hair and holding a curved stick. In his full publication of the vase, K. Schauenburg suggested that he is Atlas, who in some versions of the myth was a victim of the Gorgon's gaze and thus gave his name to a mountain. Here he would be a kind of local divinity or personification, of a type that occurs in later red-figure - usually seated and off to one side - alluding to the mountain setting.

The Nausicaa Painter is one of Beazley's "Later Mannerists." His real name is given by a signature on an amphora in London (*ARV²* 1107,7), Polygnotos, but since the name is shared by two other vase-painters, as well as the famous wall painter, the nickname taken from his painting of Odysseus and Nausicaa (*ARV²* 1107,2) has been retained.

Bibliography: Beazley, *ARV²* 1683,48*bis; Paralipomena* 452; C. Alexander, in *Art News* 61 (1962) 29; ibid., in *Arts in Virginia* 2 (1962) 9; K. Schauenburg, "Zu einer Hydria des Nausikaa-Malers in Richmond," *Kunst in Hessen und am Mittelrhein* 3 (1963) 3-15; *Ancient Art in the Virginia Museum* (Richmond 1973) 95.

detail

Cults and Festivals

As in other societies characterized by a state religion, everyday life in the Greek city-states was permeated by cult ritual and other religious activity to a much greater extent than that to which we are accustomed. Many spheres of life which seem to us entirely secular were for the Greeks integral parts of their religion. Thus, for example, the plays of the great Athenian comic and tragic dramatists were all performed at festivals in honor of Dionysos, patron god of the theatre. And all the major athletic competitions were held in panhellenic sanctuaries, of Zeus at Olympia and Nemea, Apollo at Delphi, and Poseidon at the Isthmus. With a pantheon of twelve Olympian gods and numerous minor divinities, as well as many heroes who received cult worship, Greek religion was richer and more variegated, if not usually as intense as in the Judeo-Christian tradition.

Our evidence for the cults and festivals of Athens is far more complete than for those of any other Greek city, thanks to the considerable body of surviving literary and epigraphic sources, to extensive excavation of the Agora and other parts of the ancient city, and, to some degree, to the evidence provided by many Attic vase-paintings. These sources attest to the existence in Athens of dozens of cult places in honor of most of the gods, many of the mythical ancestors of the Athenians, like Erechtheus, Kekrops (see [4]), and Theseus, of Herakles, and of various nature divinities, like Pan, the Nymphs, and the Graces. The sources also allow a reconstruction of the religious calendar of the Athenian year, with at least a couple of festivals in each of the twelve months. Among the more important of these were: the Anthesteria, in honor of Dionysos, to celebrate the first bloom of the flowers and the tasting of the new wine; the Greater Dionysia and the Lenaia, also in honor of Dionysos, at both of which dramatic contests were held; the Eleusinian Mysteries, for initiation into the cult of Demeter and Kore at Eleusis; the Thesmophoria, a festival reserved for women and associated with fertility; and, most important, the Panathenaia.

The 28th day of the month Hekatombaion (in midsummer) was celebrated as the birthday of Athena, and since she was the city goddess of Athens, this came to be the greatest festival of the Athenian year. The central event of the Panathenaia was a procession which brought a new peplos, woven during the preceding year, to drape the goddess' ancient and most holy image on the Acropolis. The procession had been instituted at least as early as the seventh century, perhaps earlier, but a major reorganization of the festival took place in 566/5. From that year the festival was designated every fourth year as the Great Panathenaia and was accompanied by several athletic contests, like those at Olympia. Prizes for victorious athletes were quantities of olive oil contained in amphoras of a special shape (see [40]), decorated with a warlike Athena on one side and the particular event on the other. Over the next half century the competition was further broadened to include recitations from Homer and musical events [40]. The Panathenaic amphoras remained constant, however, even continuing to be decorated in black-figure long after the technique had otherwise died out, down into the fourth century.

Among private religious rituals, as opposed to those sponsored by the state, the one we know most about (especially, again, in Athens) was the burial of the dead. On the day following a death, the deceased was laid out on a couch at home, the *prothesis*, and most lamentation by family and friends took place here, rather than in public. The *prothesis* is depicted on Attic Geometric vases of the eighth century and, more vividly, on black-figure plaques of the sixth. The next day the dead was conveyed to the grave site by cart, the *ekphora*, a scene shown only very rarely on Attic vases. In a simple ceremony, the body was lowered into the ground, libations poured, and the mourners returned home for a meal. But they returned every year to the tomb for annual rites, including offerings of garlands and ribbons [42-44]. Several different vase shapes were associated with funerary ritual, including the loutrophoros and lebes gamikos (for those who died unmarried). But in Classical Athens, white lekythoi, in which offerings of oil were brought to the tomb, were most characteristic, and they survive in thousands of examples [42-45].

39

Attic Red-Figure Column-Krater

Collection of the Duke University Museum of Art, Durham (1972. 1)
Attributed to a Follower of the Pan Painter [Cahn]
Ca. 470 B.C.
  Height: 30 cm.
  Diameter: 28 cm.

Side A: Youth making a sacrifice
Side B: Youth with two spits

The front of this vase (**side A**), recognizable not only by the more elaborate picture but by the lotus bud chain on the neck, shows a youth in a sanctuary in the process of making a sacrifice. All the elements of a Greek outdoor religious shrine are here: a plain rectangular altar festooned with a garland; a *pinax* or votive plaque hanging above; and a three-legged table with claw feet bearing sacrificial food (cakes or meat). In addition, the youth has a *liknon* or openwork basket cradled in his left arm; with his right hand, he seems to be reaching for something to place on the altar toward which he looks. The reverse (**side B**) has a single figure, another youth, standing in profile to the right so that he is facing the altar and the youth on the other side. He holds two long spits, used in roasting meat. The one held horizontally in his right hand already has meat adhering to the end; the one held upright in his left appears to be empty.

Not only the mannerist style but the subject matter and many of the details of the Duke krater owe much to paintings by the Pan Painter. His most famous scene of sacrifice is the Busiris pelike in Athens (Beazley, *ARV*² 554, 82) where Herakles has turned the tables on his Egyptian adversaries. One of the fleeing priests on the reverse carries a table and bundle of spits. Even more pertinent, however, is the Pan Painter's column-krater in Naples (Beazley, *ARV*² 551, 15) which depicts a shrine of Hermes. Here one youth is already roasting meat over a flaming altar, while another, half-draped like the youths on the Duke krater, looks on holding a *liknon*. Although the vase in Durham is much simpler in composition, it nonetheless conveys the essential aspects of a religious scene.

JENIFER NEILS

Bibliography: *Attische Rotfigurige Vasen*, Sonderliste N. Münzen & Medaillen, Basel, May 1971, no. 8, pp. 10ff. On meat roasting in religious scenes: G. Rizza, "Una nuova pelike a figure rosse e lo 'Splanchnoptes' di Styppax," *Annuario della Scuola Archeologica di Atene* 37-38 (1959-60) 321-345.

Side A

Side B

103

40

Attic Black-Figure Neck Amphora of Panathenaic Shape

Collection of the Archer M. Huntington Art Gallery, the University of Texas,
  Austin, James R. Dougherty, Jr. Foundation and Archer M. Huntington
  Museum Fund Purchase (1980.32)
Ca. 540 B.C.
  Height: 27.5 cm.
  Diameter: 17.2 cm.

Side A: Athena
Side B: Flute player between two judges

The vase is of the same shape as those given to victors in the Panathenaic Games, and the pose of Athena on **side A** is similar to that on prize amphoras. But this is not a prize vase, for it is too small and lacks the inscription TON AΘENEΘEN AΘΛON ("From the Games at Athens") running alongside one of the columns that flank Athena.

On side A, Athena stands in the pose of the *promachos* ("who fights in the forefront"), fully armed; she held a spear in her upraised left hand. She wears an Attic helmet, with a high crest projecting from a simple cap, a necklet, long belted peplos, and her aegis slung crosswise so that three snake heads are visible behind. Her shield, with a wide rim painted in red, has as a device three large white balls. She stands between two slender Doric columns, on top of which perch owls, in place of the cocks which regularly stand atop the columns on Panathenaic prize amphoras. The owl is Athena's (hence Athens') bird.

On side B, a young flutist (*auletes*) stands on a three-stepped podium (*bema*) and plays, while two seated figures listen. The *auletes* wears a loose fitting chiton, a fillet around his head, and a *phorbeia*, or leather mouthpiece which helps hold the flutes in place. One of the listeners is beardless, the other bearded; both sit on folding stools and wear a striped *himation* over a *chiton*.

Because of the Panathenaic context - the vase's shape and the Athena of Side A - it seems likely that the seated listeners are judges and that the scene refers to musical competitions which took place at the Greater Panathenaea in Athens every four years. Literary and epigraphical sources do not confirm the existence of such musical contests before the fourth century, but this vase and several others suggest that in the sixth and early fifth centuries there may have been as many as four musical events: flute-playing and lyre-playing, either alone or accompanying a singer (a lyre player could accompany himself). These musical competitions, along with contests for rhapsodes, who recited passages from Homer, may have all been introduced with the major reorganization of the Panathenaea in 566 B.C. The earliest of the vases, about 560, is an amphora of Panathenaic shape in London (B141), on which a flute-player and a bearded man stand facing each other on a low platform, between a young athlete and a seated judge. Perhaps this scene represents the contest for *aulodia*, singing to the flute, while ours shows *auletria*, or unaccompanied flute-playing.

Bibliography: *CVA* Castle Ashby (Great Britain 15) 8-9 and pl. 15, 5-6; *Greek, Etruscan and South Italian Vases from Castle Ashby* Sale Catalogue, Christie's, London, July 2, 1980, lot. 89, pp. 142-143, ill. E. Gerhard, in *Archaeologische Zeitung* 1846, 340, no. 2; A. Furtwaengler, *ibid*. 1881, 303; H. Philippart, in *L'Antiquité Classique* 4 (1935) 212. On musical contests at the Panathenaia: J. A. Davison, in *Journal of Hellenic Studies* 78 (1958) 36-42.

Side A

Side B

41

Attic Black-Figure Lekythos

Collection of Tulane University, Gift of Alvin P. Howard, New Orleans
Attributed to the Gela Painter [Bothmer]
Ca. 500 B.C.
      Height: 29.9 cm.
      Diameter: 12.8 cm.

Bull being led to sacrifice

Four men accompany a sacrificial bull, forming a small procession. Alongside the animal stands a man holding a vine in his left hand. He wears a fillet, and the border of his *himation* is decorated with white balls. Perhaps these trappings indicate that he is a priest. Just behind the bull walks a flute-player; next comes a man holding vines who wears a wreath of incised leaves; and finally another man holding vines. All four are bearded and wear *himatia* draped over the left shoulder.

The bull was always a favorite sacrificial victim, from Homeric times to the historic period of the sixth and fifth centuries. Like other forms of religious ritual, a sacrifice was often performed to musical accompaniment. Such processions leading sacrificial animals were, for example, a conspicuous part of the Panathenaic festival in Athens, to judge from the depiction of such a procession on the Parthenon frieze.

The Gela Painter, to whom this vase is attributed, was a prolific artist who began his career at the end of the sixth century and decorated nearly two hundred lekythoi which survive. He is known for his originality of subject matter, and this lively version of a subject not often represented in vase-painting is a good example of his work.

Bibliography: Unpublished. The Gela Painter: C.H.E. Haspels, *Attic Black-figured Lekythoi* (Paris 1936) 78-86; 205-215; Beazley, *ABV* 473-75.

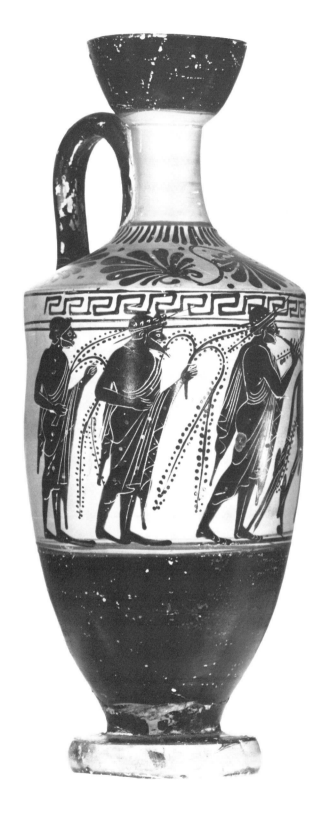

107

42

Attic White-Ground Lekythos

Private Collection, New Orleans
Attributed to the Thanatos Painter [Bothmer]
Ca. 460-450 B.C.

Height: 26.1 cm.
Diameter: 8.5 cm.

Two women mourning at a tomb

The scene shows a visit to the tomb of a loved one, the most popular subject on white-ground funerary lekythoi. In the center, the stele, crowned by a low pediment, stands on a broad two-stepped platform. Two sashes are tied around the stele, one pulled tight near the top, the other hanging loosely near the bottom. The women on either side of the stele are, unlike some in such scenes, openly mourning. The figure at left raises both hands slightly over her head. She wears a long *chiton* and a loose-fitting red *himation*. The other woman, whose hair is very closely cropped (probably in mourning), kneels beside the tomb and with both hands takes hold of the upper step. She looks down at the stone with intent but calm gaze. She too wears a *chiton* and red *himation*, the latter having fallen off her shoulder to her waist.

White-ground lekythoi were first produced in the late sixth century [26], and for several generations they were decorated with a wide variety of subjects and were presumably used, in the home and elsewhere, like black- or red-figure lekythoi, as oil containers. In the Early Classical period, white lekythoi began to assume a specialized function as offerings for the dead, placed on or in the tomb. The delicate nature of the white paint and the fugitive colors that were often applied made these vases somewhat impractical for everyday use and perhaps helped suggest this ritual purpose.

This vase, like the two which follow, is the work of the Thanatos Painter, one of the small number of fine painters who decorated exclusively white lekythoi in the middle years of the fifth century. He was strongly influenced by the Achilles Painter, the greatest vase-painter of the day, but, unlike him, did not, as far as we know, also work in red-figure. He is also one of the first painters whose white lekythoi are, to judge from the iconography, entirely funerary. Nearly fifty white lekythoi are attributed to the Thanatos Painter, who is named for a rare representation of Thanatos and Hypnos (Death and Sleep) on a lekythos in London (Beazley, *ARV²* 1228, 12).

The shoulders of Classical white lekythoi are regularly decorated with a pattern of three palmettes linked by spiralling tendrils. Within this scheme many subtle variations can be detected from painter to painter; the Thanatos Painter generally favors a simple pattern which is uncluttered by many extra tendrils and lotus buds. On most of his lekythoi, the figures are outlined in dilute glaze of lustrous golden brown or yellow, but in a few of his later works, including these three, he adopts the new technique of outline in matte paint, red or black, or a mixture of the two. The figures on this vase are more slender than most by the Thanatos painter, and Beazley was uncertain whether this might be the work of a pupil.

Bibliography: Unpublished. Beazley, *ARV²* 1230, 46. On the Thanatos Painter: D. C. Kurtz, *Athenian White Lekythoi* (Oxford 1975) 38-41.

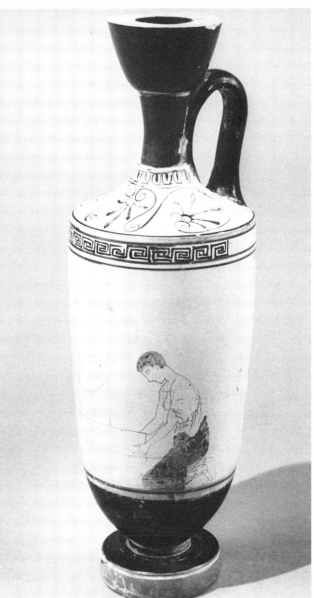

Detail of Shoulder

109

43

Attic White-Ground Lekythos

Private Collection, New Orleans
Attributed to the Thanatos Painter [Bothmer]
Ca. 460-450 B.C.
  Height: 25.8 cm.
  Diameter: 8.5 cm.

Woman and little girl at a tomb

In the center, the plain shaft of the stele stands on a tall, wide base. Sashes hang loosely near the top. A young girl approaches the tomb from the left, holding out a doll in both hands. She has curly hair and wears a very thin, transparent *chiton*. Her features are those of an adult, but her stature - more than a head shorter than the woman opposite - indicates that she is meant to be a child. As on the preceding vase, the scene is a visit to the tomb of a family member, and the doll is a gift for the deceased, a token of remembrance. Curiously, the doll bears a strong resemblance to the girl who carries it. Perhaps the tomb is a child's, as is certainly the case on the lekythos which follows.

The woman at the right stands frontally, her head in profile looking toward the tomb. With her right hand she gestures toward the stele, or past it to the girl, and in her left she holds a basket which probably contains sashes, like the chest on [44]. Behind the girl is a conical object with zig-zag decoration and two long strings, suspended from the upper border of the picture field. It is a *sakkos*, or snood, a kind of hairnet often worn by women or seen hanging on the wall in domestic scenes.

This lekythos and two others from the same collection are all attributed to the Thanatos Painter (see [43]).

Bibliography: Unpublished. Beazley, *ARV*² 1230, 45.

detail

111

44

Attic White-Ground Lekythos

Private Collection, New Orleans
Attributed to the Thanatos Painter [Bothmer]
Ca. 460-450 B.C.
    Height: 25.7 cm.
    Diameter: 8.3 cm.

Woman and maid at a child's tomb

The tomb consists of a short, nearly square stele on top of a high four-stepped podium. Several red sashes are tied around the stele and others trail down the steps. Atop the stele sits a pudgy little boy, scarcely more than a baby, with tousled curly hair. This has been called a statue of the dead child, though it is extremely lifelike. It could represent an image of the deceased as in life, just as on later white lekythoi a dead warrior is sometimes seen sitting on the steps of his own tomb [45].

A servant girl, with close-cropped hair, snub nose, full lips, and prominent chin, approaches from the right, holding out an alabastron in her left hand. Clearly she is meant to be a Negro. On her head she carries a long, low basket of sashes like those already decorating the tomb. At the left stands a woman closely wrapped in a dark red cloak, perhaps the mother of the dead child. Behind her hangs a *sakkos* (see [43]).

The vase is by the Thanatos Painter, to whom the previous two lekythoi from the same collection are also attributed [42, 43].

detail

Bibliography: Unpublished. *ARV²* 1230,44. for the Negro maid, compare a lekythos by the Bosanquet Painter, Berlin inv. 3291; *ARV²* 1227,9; F. M. Snowden, *Blacks in Antiquity* (Cambridge, Mass. 1970) fig. 25.

45

Attic White-Ground Lekythos

Collection of Mr. and Mrs. Arthur Q. Davis, New Orleans
Unattributed
Ca. 430-420 B.C.
>Height: 40 cm.
>Diameter: 10.9 cm.

Warrior and woman at tomb

In the center stands a tall stele on a low two-stepped base. Two dark blue ribbons are hung around it, and it is crowned by sketchy floral ornaments. At the right sits a young beardless warrior. He wears a short belted tunic which is fastened at the left shoulder and a dark blue *chlamys*. The latter is fastened by a brooch over his chest and flows down his back, so that he sits on the lower part of it. He also appears to have a hat resting on the nape of the neck, perhaps a *petasos*, and he holds two spears in his raised left hand.

From the left side approaches a woman in a thin, frilly *chiton*. She holds a small basket by its arching handle in her left hand and a phiale in her right.

The motif of a dead young warrior sitting on or beside his own tomb occurs on white lekythoi of the last third of the fifth century. One particularly well known example, belonging to Group R, is in the National Museum, Athens (Beazley, *ARV²* 1383, 11). Many of these must have been made for the families of those who fell in the Peloponnesian War. The woman bringing offerings to the grave could be the deceased young man's mother, sister, or wife.

Bibliography: New Orleans Museum of Art, *New Orleans Collects*, 1971, no. 287.

War and Combat

Warfare between neighboring states was an almost constant feature of Greek life during much of the Archaic and Classical periods. Only on one occasion did all the Greeks unite to defend themselves against a common enemy from outside - the Persians - in 490 and again in 480/79. Most of the time war resulted from one city's attempt to assert its hegemony in a particular region, to settle an old grudge, or to take advantage of a temporarily weakened neighbor. Defensive alliances were rapidly formed among states, then as rapidly abrogated and reformed in different alignments. The most devastating instance of such civil strife was the Peloponnesian War, which was essentially a struggle between two cities, Athens and Sparta, for supremacy in Greece, but, as it dragged on for 27 years (431-404), eventually drew in almost every other Greek city and was played out on battlefields all over the country.

There were many good precedents for this constant aggression in the heroic myths of the Greeks. The greatest of all the sagas told the story of a bloody and protracted ten-year war at Troy. That was an instance of Greeks allied against a foreign enemy, as in the Persian Wars, to which it was sometimes likened in the Early Classical period (see J. Boardman, in *Antike Kunst* 19 [1976] 3-18). But warfare between Greek cities is also a frequent element in heroic legend, and Bronze Age archaeology has confirmed that raids on neighboring citadels and piracy on land and sea were a way of life for the earliest mainland Greeks, whose society is mirrored in the myths.

Greek art reflects this preoccupation with war, often on a grand scale. From the later sixth century on, there is scarcely a single Greek temple that did not include among its sculptural decoration - pediments, frieze, metopes - at least one large scale battle scene - Greeks against Amazons, Lapiths against Centaurs, Greeks against Trojans, to name the most often represented. Monumental wall painting, now regrettably all lost, provided an ideal medium for battle scenes on an epic scale which vase-painters could never hope to duplicate. Yet the vases also depict an endless variety of warfare, from single combat to full scale engagement, and provide some of our best documentation both for mythological battles and for military equipment and practises in the historical period.

It is not always easy to distinguish between a vase-painting of a battle scene set in the Heroic Age, between Greeks and Trojans for example, and one which is meant to depict contemporary Greeks. By convention Greek art avoided representing actual historical events, such as battles, which

had been so conspicuous a feature of the art of the ancient Near East and would be again in Roman art. There are, for example, no identifiable depictions of an episode from the Peloponnesian War, and even the victory over the Persians, Greece's proudest moment, was seldom shown. But many battle scenes which are not recognizably mythological may well be generic scenes, not of a particular battle, but still accurate in details of warfare as it was practiced in the painter's own day.

Part of the difficulty in separating the historical from the mythological stems from the consistency of much Greek armor from the Bronze and Iron Ages, known to us best from Homer's descriptions, corroborated by archaeological finds, to the Classical period. A second difficulty is that the vase-painters did not know any more about Bronze Age arms and armor than we do and instead outfitted their heroic subjects in contemporary style. For a heavily armed infantryman, called by the Greeks a hoplite, this consisted of a helmet, cuirass (corselet), greaves (shin-guards), shield, sword, and one or two spears. The boar's tusk helmet of the Homeric poems was replaced by one of bronze, sometimes with a ridge extending over the middle of the cap and sometimes with a tall crest attached [35, 49]. Helmets shown on Greek vases are usually of one of two types: Attic, with only a cap resting on the forehead, leaving the face exposed [4, 40]; and Corinthian, with wide cheekpieces and noseguard, almost entirely covering the face [3]. The corselet could be of leather or bronze, in either case two pieces, for front and back, fastened at the shoulders and below. This came only to the waist and was worn over a kind of short skirt (*chiton*) woven of especially strong threads. The greaves were bronze, but slightly elastic, so they could be pulled on over the knee and fastened at the ankle. The shields of the Heroic Age, whether the so-called figure-of-eight or the tower shield, were enormous, covering most of the body, and made of bull's hide, perhaps covered with bronze. Historical shields, some of which have been found, were round or oval and considerable smaller, though still extremely heavy in bronze.

Once hoplite warfare was introduced in the seventh century, most engagements took place on foot. Light armed troops included archers [2], who were sometimes foreign mercenaries. Cavalry was also used, but was limited to those men with enough wealth to provide their own horse. Fighting from chariots was not practised in the historical period, and in fact four-horse chariots, such as are seen so often on vases [48, 49], were probably not used in military context at all. Thus their appearance on vases must be understood as an allusion to the mythical past.

46

Early Corinthian Aryballos

Collection of the Archer M. Huntington Art Gallery, the University of Texas,
   Austin, James R. Dougherty, Jr. Foundation and Archer M. Huntington
   Museum Fund Purchase (1980.37)
Warrior Group
Ca. 600 B.C.
      Height: 6.2 cm.

Duel of warriors flanked by riders

The incision and attention to detail are particularly careful on this miniature Corinthian perfume bottle. The two warriors on foot are heraldically posed, and the two squires who wait behind them are also perfectly symmetrical. Only the contrast between the two shields which occupy the center of the composition, one seen from the outside, the other from the inside, mitigates the rigid symmetry.

The combatants are dressed alike in low crested Corinthian helmets, short tunics with decorated border at top and bottom, and greaves. Subtle variations in the incised decoration of the helmet crests and the borders of the garments also enliven the composition. They fight with spears, though the right hand warrior's weapon is mostly obscured behind his body and shield. The other warrior's spear crosses behind his head, an impossible position, in order not to block our view of his profile. The one shield device we can see is a splendid frontal bull's head which fills the surface and even overlaps the rim. The horsemen also wear tunics, though undecorated, and fillets in their long flowing hair.

The rest of the vase's surface is almost covered with filling ornament, mostly plain blobs and rosettes whose incision is not always as careful as that of the figures. In addition there is a pattern of tongues on the shoulder and the lip, and an incised double palmette on the handle.

The footless round aryballos became a very popular shape rather suddenly in the Early Corinthian period, at the end of the seventh century, perhaps due to contact with the Near East, where the shape had long been known. By about 600, the animal style that had dominated earlier Corinthian vase-painting was starting to die out, and a figured style, favoring soldiers, horsemen, and padded dancers, was increasingly popular. The warrior Group comprises several dozen aryballoi of Payne's shape B1. Although the Austin vase is unattributed, according to D. A. Amyx the style recalls the Heraldic Riders Painter.

Bibliography: D. A. Amyx, *Corinthian Vase-Painting of the Archaic Period* (Berkeley: in press, 1981) 309, 11 *bis*; *CVA* Castle Ashby (Great Britain 15) 19 and pl. 30, 4-6; *Greek, Etruscan and South Italian Vases from Castle Ashby* Sale Catalogue, Christie's, London, July 2, 1980, lot. 54ii, p. 95, ill. On the Warrior Group: H. Payne, *Necrocorinthia* (Oxford 1931) 288.

47

Attic Red-Figure Oinochoe

Collection of the North Carolina Museum of Art, Raleigh (G. 79. 11. 5)
Attributed to the Painter of the Brussels Oinochoai
Ca. 470-460 B. C.

Height: 24.5 cm.
Diameter: 15.25 cm.

Two warriors

Lacking all subsidiary ornament, this sleek, black-glazed oinochoe highlights two confronted warriors. The one to the left is older, bearded, and ready for battle. He is dressed in a short *chiton*, cuirass and Corinthian helmet, and armed with a spear and large circular shield, the device of which is a writhing black snake. Standing frontally, he gazes to his left at the youth on the other side of the vase. This warrior is less well equipped. Despite a cloth headband, his long hair lies in ringlets over his shoulders. His nude body is draped with a long *chlamys* or cloak. He holds a spear and a plain black shield in his left hand, and holds forth a crested Corinthian helmet in his right.

The two warriors are certainly related in some way. Not only do they stare at each other, but on similarly shaped vases the two sides are usually connected. It has been suggested that the younger warrior is receiving arms from the older in preparation for the Persian Wars which ended in 480/479 B. C. However, arming scenes are ubiquitous in Attic vase-painting, and this particular one is likely to be simply genre.

On the other hand, the shape of this footless oinochoe is very rare in Attica, although popular with the Etruscans. Hence, it and the others by the Painter of the Brussels Oinochoai may well have been made for export.

JENIFER NEILS

Bibliography: North Carolina Museum of Art, *Calendar* (January, 1980). For other spouted oinochoai: K. Schauenburg, "ΕΥΡΥΜΕΔΩΝ ΕΙΜΙ" *Mitteilungen des Deutschen Archäologischen Instituts, Athenische Abteilung* 90 (1975) 97-102. On oinochoai: J. R. Green, "Oinochoe," *Bulletin of the Institute of Classical Studies* 19 (1972) 1-16. On the Painter of the Brussels Oinochoai: Beazley, *ARV²* 775.

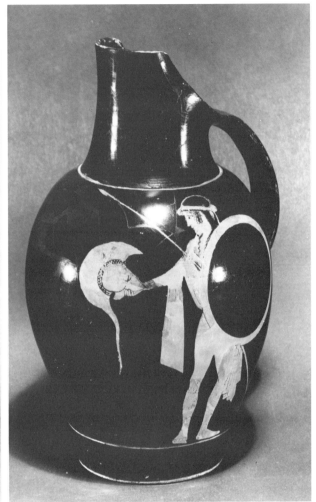

48

Attic Black-Figure Neck-Amphora

Collection of the John and Mable Ringling Museum of Art, Sarasota, Gift of
    Mr. Manuel Ortiz, Jr., (1600. G4)
Attributed to the Edinburgh Painter [Bothmer]
Ca. 500-480 B. C.
    Height: 26.9 cm.
    Diameter: 16.9 cm.

Side A: Goddess and warrior in a wheeling chariot
Side B: Two warriors leaving home

A four-horse chariot wheeling round is a favorite subject on late black-figure vases, mainly neck-amphoras. **On side A**, the two horses on the far side raise their forelegs high in the air, creating a whirl of movement, and each horse's head is seen from a different angle, the middle two meeting or overlapping. In the car stand a female figure, holding the reins, and beside her a warrior in a high crested helmet, holding a spear. Often when the driver of a chariot is female, she is Athena, recognizable by her helmet. Without the helmet, we must assume she is another goddess, but cannot say which one (compare the neck-amphora in the Agora: Beazley, *Paralipomena* 302).

On side B, two young, fully-armed warriors prepare to depart for battle. They wear greaves and Corinthian helmets, one with a low crest, the other a high one. They stand in profile to left so that their shield devices are visible: a facing bull's head and two balls (a third ball is presumably hidden behind the other shield). One warrior carries a spear and a second cuts diagonally across the pair. The warriors stand between an older man and a woman: perhaps two brothers taking leave of their parents. The old man is bearded and balding, though his hair is long in back. He wears a *chiton* and *himation* and leans on a staff. The woman wears a fillet, and her *chiton* is decorated at the neck and the hem.

The Edinburgh Painter, perhaps best known for his innovation in the use of white-ground [26], also decorated many small neck-amphoras in the conventional black-figure technique.

Bibliography: Unpublished. For similar neck-amphoras by the Edinburgh Painter:
Beazley, *ABV* 478 (iii).

Side A

Side B

49

Attic Black-Figure Kyathos

Collection of the Duke University Museum of Art, Durham (1969.3).
Ca. 510-500 B. C.

Height: 17 cm.
Diameter: 16 cm.

Fight with Chariots

The composition forms a continuous frieze around the outer surface of the vase. At the center, where a large portion is unfortunately missing, two heavily armed warriors (hoplites) do battle. The figure moving toward the right has the upper hand, a convention in Greek art, as his opponent sinks to his knees. The inside of the victor's shield is seen, his left arm holding it through a strap (porpax). Behind each warrior is his four-horse chariot; in the car stands the charioteer wearing the traditional long white chiton. The scene is flanked by two onlookers, one on either side of the handle: an armed hoplite and a nude figure with a cloak draped over one arm.

Chariots were not used in Greek warfare in the historical period. Homeric heroes do, however, regularly ride to the field of battle in a chariot, often accompanied by a charioteer, then dismount to fight in single combat. Thus this scene was probably inspired by epic poetry, though without other clues it is impossible to try to name the combatants.

The kyathos is a small dipper with a single high-swung handle, used for ladling wine out of a krater. The shape is an adaptation of an Etruscan vessel which had been made in Italy as early as the seventh century. Its manufacture began in Athens about 535 B. C. and continued for only a half century, apparently intended exclusively for export to Etruria.

Most of the roughly 450 extant kyathoi seem to have been produced by one large workshop in the Athenian potters' quarter, that of Nikosthenes, which also manufactured other shapes for export to Etruria. The majority of kyathoi are decorated with Dionysiac subjects, a reference to the vessel's association with wine. Scenes of combat are relatively rare: four kyathoi by the Philon Painter depict fight scenes (Beazley, *ABV* 516-517; *Paralipomena* 255), including horsemen, but none other has chariots.

Bibliography: *Hesperia Art Bulletin* 45/46 (January, 1969) A15. On kyathoi: M. M. Eisman, "Attic Kyathos Production," *Archaeology* 28 (1975) 76-83.

Everyday Life

One of the paradoxes of Greek life is that in Athens of the Classical period, marked as it was by such high achievements in the arts and a noble experiment in a democratic form of government, the treatment of women was more repressive and unenlightened than at almost any other time and place in the history of the West. Girls of citizen families were married off at an early age (see p. 157), thus denying them the oppportunity for the rigorous education - physical, intellectual, and musical - to which a boy's adolescence was dedicated. Once installed in her new home, a woman's responsibilities were the care of children and the supervison of the household. At no time, either before or after marriage, was it considered proper for a woman to leave the house by herself or in the company of other women, except on rare occasions such as religious festivals. This virtual seclusion is reminiscent of that which we associate with the East, particularly the countries of Islam. Even within the home, life was unusually limited, and a wife could not expect to see much of her husband, as dining and sleeping quarters were separate. A couple often did not know each other before their marriage, and it is unlikely in most cases that much intimacy developed afterwards.

Athenian men, on the other hand, led very public lives centered in the Agora, the meeting place of the assembly and the law courts and hub of commercial transactions. On any given day, many hundreds of men would swarm to the law courts alone, since a typical jury numbered 501. Wealthy men, mainly landowners, were free to wander further afield, frequenting the gymnasium and palestra, whiling away the day in conversation as many Greek men do in cafés nowadays. The men of the middle class, tradesmen and artisans (including a sizeable number of potters and painters), were of course busy during the day working in the commercial districts around the Agora, such as the Kerameikos (potter's quarter).

This great disparity between the lives of women and men was made possible in part by the institution of slavery, another paradoxical aspect of the first western democracy. Even a family of moderate means could usually afford one or more household slaves, who labored under the watchful eye of the mistress and performed tasks outside the house - fetching water at a public fountain house (a favorite scene on black-figure vases), buying groceries, escorting boys to and from school. The mistress devoted herself to those tasks that could be done in the home, especially the weaving of clothing [51-52].

Not surprisingly, the classical literature of Athens, all of it written by men, tells us little about the private domestic lives of women. By contrast, Attic vase-paintings, which give us only occasional glimpses of the daily activities of men - a rare scene of a potter's shop, a shoemaker, a foundry - depict in minute detail and in hundreds of examples the routine lives of women at home. The obvious explanation is that several pottery shapes were intended primarily for use by women: the lekythos [52] and its variant, the squat lekythos [50], to hold oil, unguent, or perfume; the pyxis and lekanis, round boxes to hold toiletries. These shapes, together with the picture of women's lives that their decoration affords, belong primarily to the second half of the fifth century. It has often been suggested that the "feminization" of the vase-painters' repertoire in this period reflects a kind of escapism from the relentless atrocities and suffering of the Peloponnesian War which filled so many of those years.

When women are not engaged in working wool, they are seen most often bathing, dressing, and attending to their make-up and coiffure [50]. Considering how seldom women ever left the house, they do seem to spend an inordinate amount of time on such activities, and it is doubtful that they are beautifying themselves in preparation for their husbands' return from work.

Though children are not generally a favorite subject in Greek art and were seldom convincingly rendered before the mid-fifth century [44], they are not entirely neglected either. In the Archaic period they probably amused themselves mainly with pets and other animals [53], but by the later fifth century they enjoyed a full range of toys and games, many of which are depicted on vases. Many of their toys *were* vases, miniature versions of standard shapes, or objects such as knucklebones which were translated into ceramic imitations.

50

Attic Red-Figure Squat Lekythos

Collection of Ackland Art Museum, University of North Carolina,
    Chapel Hill (71.8.1)
Manner of the Eretria Painter [A. Lezzi-Hafter]
Ca. 430-420 B.C.
        Height: 21.3 cm.
        Diameter: 14.6 cm.

Women at their toilette

Seventeen women sit or stand in a variety of poses, in two registers, each holding an attribute which figured in the daily life of Athenian matrons and their maid-servants.

The figures are grouped in pairs, each consisting of a mistress and maid, with the exception of one three-some in the upper register: a seated mistress attended by two standing maids (drawing, pps. 130-131, nos. 3, 4, 5). Many poses are similar, but none exactly duplicates another, and variations in dress, coiffure, and attributes also help avoid monotony.

The most frequent attribute is a small chest or box, held by six of the figures (2, 5, 7, 10, 12, 15). Most of these chests are made of wicker and could have contained jewelry, toiletries, wool, articles of clothing, or other objects. They vary in size and shape: three have legs (5, 7, 12) and of these one has animal feet (12). Some are richly patterned on the outside (2, 10), others plain. On one can be seen two round knobs (5), which look like drawer pulls, but are probably for tying on the lid. Other attributes are a wicker wool basket (9), a ball of wool (11), mirrors (4, 13, 17), an alabastron for precious oil or perfume (8), leafy sprigs (1, 14), and an embroidered headband with tasseled fringe (16). In addition two objects are suspended from the wall behind: a headband (between 9 and 10) and an alabastron (between 3 and 4). This bottle, like the one held by a seated mistress (8), is made of glass, decorated with a multi-colored zig-zag pattern, a type

which has survived in several examples.

Four of the women sit on *klismoi*, backed chairs with curving legs (4, 6, 11, 14; compare the Chapel Hill lekythos, [52]). One sits on a four-legged stool, a *diphros* (8). Most of the maids wear only a thin, crinkly linen garment, the *chiton* (e.g. 5), while several of the matrons wear a heavy woolen peplos (2, 16). Some wear both a *chiton* and, over it, a *himation* (e.g. 4). Most of the women wear their hair up and bound with a headband, or *mitra*, which may be patterned (5, 12). Only one mistress' hair hangs down in loose wavy tresses (6); perhaps she will use the contents of the chest being handed to her to tie it up.

Squat lekythoi were first manufactured in Athens earlier in the fifth century and were especially popular during the period of this vase. They were used to contain oil and were primarily for use at home by women like those depicted on this example.

In style the vase is closely related to the work of the Eretria Painter, the greatest miniaturist of his genera-tion. The disposition of the figures in superposed registers is unusual and is paralleled by only two other squat lekythoi, one by the Eretria Painter (Beazley, *ARV²* 1248, 9), the other by an imitator (Beazley, *ARV²* 1257, middle, 1). Originally attributed to the painter himself, the Chapel Hill vase is now consi-dered to be more likely by an imitator closely as-sociated with his workshop.

Bibliography: R. F. Sutton, Jr., "Athenian Red-Figure Lekythos by the Eretria Painter," *Ackland Notes* 8 (Chapel Hill 1972); C. R. Mack, *Classical Art from Carolina Collections* (Columbia, S.C. 1974) 22-23. On the Eretria Painter: C. Isler-Kerényi, in *Zur griechischen Kunst* (*Antike Kunst* Beiheft 9, 1972) 30-31. Attribution: A. Lezzi-Hafter, letter to R. F. Sutton, 1/28/74, and letter from R. F. Sutton to the writer, 2/25/81.

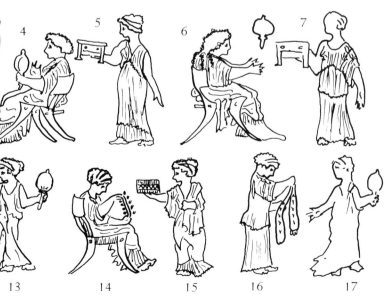

4   5   6   7

13   14   15   16   17

51

Attic Red-Figure Hydria

Collection of The Museum of Fine Arts, Houston, Museum Purchase with funds
    donated by General and Mrs. Maurice Hirsch (80.95)
Attributed to the Painter of the Yale Oinochoe
Ca. 470-460 B.C.
       Height: 34.8 cm.
       Diameter: 33.3 cm.

Women working wool

The scene is a charming and authentic image of Athenian domestic life, showing three young women and a pet heron. In the center, a woman stands over a *kalathos*, a wicker wool basket, about to place in it (or take from it) a large bundle of wool. (Compare the woman drawing skeins of wool from a *kalathos* on the Chapel Hill lekythos [52]). At the left a woman holds an alabastron, an unguent bottle, in one hand, and in the other reaches out a similar bottle over the stooping figure, toward a third woman at the right. The women at left and right wear plain *chiton* and *himation*, while the central figure's garment is gaily decorated with an all-over pattern and fringed hem. All three wear a fillet, and their hair is tied in a knot at the back.

A heron, standing on long spindly legs, faces and watches intently the woman in the center. The heron was sacred to Aphrodite and was a favorite pet of Athenian matrons. Hence it is seen not infrequently in domestic settings such as this one.

Scenes of women working wool, as well as other domestic occupations, become increasingly popular in Attic red-figure after about 500 B.C. Of six hydrias attributed to the Painter of the Yale Oinochoe, five, including this one, show women's scenes with common elements. A hydria in Copenhagen (Beazley, *ARV*² 503, 24) portrays another aspect of wool working, a woman holding spindle and distaff. Two others, in London (503, 23) and at Harvard (503, 22), include herons, one being fed by its mistress. On the Harvard vase, a *kalathos* hangs upside down on the wall. A hydria at San Simeon (503, 21) shows a rare scene of women working out of doors, picking apples. The painter also decorated many other shapes, but his drawing is seldom as fine as it is here.

Bibliography: Unpublished. On the Painter of the Yale Oinochoe: Beazley, *ARV*² 501-503; H. M. Fracchia, in *California Studies in Classical Antiquity* 5 (1972) 103-111. On herons: J. D. Beazley, *The Lewes House Collection of Ancient Gems* (Oxford 1920) 60-61.

133

52

Attic Red-Figure Lekythos

Collection of the Ackland Art Museum, University of North Carolina, Chapel Hill (78. 15. 1)
Attributed to the Bowdoin Painter
Ca. 470-450 B. C.
>Height: 27.8 cm.
>Diameter: 9.5 cm.

Woman at a wool basket

A favorite subject of the Bowdoin Painter is a domestic scene of a woman, wearing a thin *chiton*, seated or, as here, standing near a wool basket (*kalathos*) from which she draws skeins of wool. The scene is, in Miss Richter's words, "a simple Greek version of the later Dutch interiors representing women at work" (*Attic Red-Figured Vases* [New Haven 1958] 75).

This vase includes more details of the indoor setting than most. Beside the woman is an unusually large high-backed chair, a *klismos*, with a cover spread over the seat. Two black squares mark the points at which the frame-pieces are mortised into the legs. The chair, however, is peculiarly tall and out of proportion, the back-board so high that it would function rather as a headrest. Behind the *klismos* a garment is suspended from the wall, and at the right hangs a footed basket for flowers or fruit. The tall *kalathos* is probably made of wicker.

The Bowdoin Painter was a prolific, though generally uninspired artist to whom over 200 lekythoi are attributed, as well as a small number of vases of other shapes. He had a long career, beginning at the very end of the Archaic period and extending down to at least 450.

Bibliography: Unpublished. Beazley, *ARV*² 681, 82. On *klismoi*: G. M. A. Richter, *Ancient Furniture* (Oxford 1926) 45-53.

53

Attic Black-Figure Little Master Cup

Collection of Mr. and Mrs. Edward L. Diefenthal, Metairie, Louisiana
Attributed to the Centaur Painter [Cahn]
Ca. 540 B.C.
> Height: 9.7 cm.
> Diameter (without handles): 13.7 cm.

Sides A and B: Hare hunt

The same scene is repeated without variation on both sides of the exterior of this charming small cup. A youth strides to the left, preparing to throw a stone at a large rabbit. The youth is nude but for a *chlamys* which is draped over his outstretched left arm and is decorated with a border of white dots. The rabbit is some distance away and seems as yet unaware of the danger as he hops along briskly. The rabbit's neck and flank, the youth's hair, and his *chlamys* are all painted in added red.

Rabbits were favorite pets of Athenian boys, to judge from their popularity on vases as gifts from an older man to his beloved. In addition, the hunting of wild rabbits, as here, was a popular sport among boys and young men.

The Diefenthal cup is one of a large group of small black-figure cups, decorated in miniature style, of the second and third quarters of the sixth century, named by Beazley Little Master Cups. This one is a band cup, so named from the reserved band at handle level within which the figured scene is placed. The Centaur Painter, who decorated at least twenty-five small cups and no other shapes, favored centaurs, either alone or in combat or, once, throwing a stone at a fawn (Beazley, *Paralipomena* 78, 3*bis*), a scene not unlike this one.

Bibliography: *Antike Vasen* (Sale Catalogue, Münzen und Medaillen, Basel 1977) no. 23, ill. On the Centaur Painter: Beazley, *ABV* 189-90; *Paralipomena* 78-79; F. Villard, "Le Peintre des Centaurs," in *Studies Presented to David M. Robinson* ii (St. Louis 1953) 65 - 69.

Side A

Side B

54

Attic Black-Figure "Sprinkler" (Klepsydra?)

Collection of The University Museums, University of Mississippi, Phase I
   Cultural Center (77.3.74)
Unattributed
Ca. 500 B.C.
   Height: 17.3 cm.
   Diameter: 12.2 cm.

Side A: Boy in tree; youth and man dancing
Side B: The like

The general meaning of the scene repeated on both sides of this unusual vessel is clear: the trees are fruit trees, which the boys have climbed to pick or shake down the fruit, while youths and men dance under the trees. It is harder to say what kind of fruit is meant; the shape and foliage of the trees are entirely conventional, and the painter did not bother to distinguish leaves from fruit. Dancers are common in scenes of the grape harvest, but these are clearly trees, not vines. The most probable answer is olive trees, since the olive was the fruit most highly valued by the Greeks, both as food and for its oil. The older dancers wear wreaths of leaves on their heads; the younger ones have red garlands or fillets around their heads and necks. This must be a harvest or first-fruits festival, one of those rustic, cheerful jollifications that were celebrated in villages all over the Greek-speaking world, rather than a more formal city ceremony. The dancers have slung their cloaks over their outstretched left arms, to free their legs for more energetic movement as the line of dancers goes stamping, kicking and spinning through the olive grove in one of the vigorous dances that Greek villagers enjoy to this day.

The shape of the vase is unusual and raises questions about its use. It is derived from the mastos, a cup in the shape of a human breast. The body is a sphere, topped by a clay nipple painted red. The base is pierced with some 60 small holes, and the hollow handle opens at each end into the body. In the top of the handle is a single hole; when the vessel has been filled by plunging it into a liquid, the user's thumb over the hole prevents the liquid from running out until desired. This could have been used as a sprinkler for ritual lustrations and purifications or to lift wine from a large container without disturbing the lees or bringing with it any foreign matter that might be present; it holds enough to fill a medium-sized kylix, or two small ones. If the shape has any significance for the use, it would suit both purposes: the breast has connotations of fertility for a harvest festival, or eroticism for a drinking party. The type of vessel is rare but not unique; some 5th-century examples are copied from animal-head rhyta, drinking vessels which may have a small hole in the bottom. Such rhyta may have been used to aerate wine by releasing it in a thin stream into a cup, and this may be the purpose of our "spinkler" as well. Indeed, it would be more efficient than a rhyton, releasing the wine in 60 thin streams instead of just one.

LUCY TURNBULL

Bibliography: CVA Robinson Collection 3, pl. 3,1. For rhyta as aerators of wine: H. Hoffmann, "The Persian Origin of Attic Rhyta," *Antike Kunst* 4 (1961), 21-26.

Side A

Side B

Bottom

Sports

Physical strength and athletic prowess were as much prized by the Greeks as intellectual or artistic achievement. In Athens, however, this was true only for men - thus on Attic vases only young men are seen in training and engaging in athletic contests - though in other parts of Greece, notably in Sparta, girls also took exercise out of doors.

Chariot races and other athletic competitions are already a conspicuous feature of the world of the Homeric poems, especially in the form of funeral games for a dead hero. The games for Patroklos, which Homer describes in the twenty-third book of the *Iliad*, include a chariot race, wrestling, a foot race, an archery contest, and others. In the *Odyssey* (Book Seven), the young men of Phaeacia, where the shipwrecked Odysseus has been washed ashore, challenge him to join in their athletic contests.

In historical times, the games at Olympia were thought to have originated in 776 B.C., and by the sixth century panhellenic games were held regularly at other sanctuaries: Delphi, Nemea, and the Isthmus of Corinth. The earliest competitions at Olympia were in running and wrestling, but gradually other events were added: races for both chariots and single horses, races in armor (*hoplitodromos*), the pentathlon (wrestling, running, jumping, discus, and javelin), boxing, and pankration (a no-holds-barred combination of wrestling and boxing).

In Athens, starting in the year 566 B.C., many of these same events formed part of the games at the celebration of the Greater Panathenaia every four years (see p. 101 and [40]). Competitors were divided into three classes - boys, beardless youths, men - and in addition to foot races, the pentathlon, wrestling, boxing, pankration, and a full program of horse and chariot races, there were other competitions unparalleled at Olympia. There was javelin-throwing from horseback, a torch race (*lampadedromia*), and, among team events, Pyrrhic dances (performed in armor), a regatta in the harbor of Athens, and one called simply *euandria* ("manly excellence"), which probably involved various tests of strength.

In Classical Athens, athletic training was one of the three main areas of a boy's education, along with letters and music. He probably spent his earliest years learning to read and write, from a *grammatistes*, then learning to play the lyre, from a *kitharistes*. Then, from about age 14, he went daily to the palestra (from the root *pale*, 'wrestling') of a *paidotribes*, or professional trainer, to practice not only wrestling, but running, jumping, and other sports. Most exercise could be performed in the palestra itself, a series of rooms opening off an open courtyard - except running, for which the boys would be taken to a stadium. The freeborn youth was escorted to the palestra by a family slave, his *paidagogos*, an older man who is sometimes seen in vase-paintings waiting for his charge. Once there, the boy undressed (all exercise was done in the nude), bathed, and rubbed himself with oil. A variety of paraphernalia is often pictured in palestra scenes on painted vases: sponges for washing, little cylindrical alabastra which contain oil, bronze strigils for scraping off the oil [57]. Wrestling, the competitive sport *par excellence*, is done under the watchful eye of the *paidotribes*, who usually wears a cloak and carries a long forked stick, for chastising lazy or unruly boys [60]. Jumpers always use *halteres*, a set of curved bronze weights, one swung in each hand, to increase momentum and thus extend the length of the jump [61]. The palestra employed a flute-player, who set the rhythm for all exercise. Apart from him and the paidagogoi, grown men were banned from the palestra, in some periods on pain of death, to protect the young athletes from the amorous attentions of their elders. A boy completed his physical training at age 18, when he became an ephebe and began his military service.

55

Boeotian Black-Figure Tripod-Kothon

Collection of Norbert Schimmel, courtesy of the Dallas Museum of Fine Arts
Attributed to the Boeotian Dancers Group
570-560 B. C.

Height: 13.6 cm.
Width: 18.4 cm.

Komasts, athletes, and animals

Six nude male figures are disposed in pairs on the three leg panels. The first set is engaged in a heated dance. These frolicking acrobats are komasts, comic dancers whose activities incline toward mischief-making at every opportunity. The two bearded dancers here confront each other in their jubilation. Each dancer has an incised line across the left bicep, creating the impression of a short-sleeved garment. This is a sure indication that members of this tribe of revelers were once clad, as indeed they were in earlier scenes on Attic and Corinthian komos vases from which the Boeotian komasts derive. The heavier komast gingerly raises an inviting hand to the chin of his companion in hopes of obtaining even a more intimate response. Homosexual activity is frequently depicted in scenes on Greek vases [62, 64] and especially among the ranks of komasts. Moving counterclockwise around the vase the next pair of komasts is actively engaged in another favorite pastime, the consumption of wine. The eager drinker on the right raises a wine pitcher, an oinochoe, directly to his lips. Sparing no time for the formalities of proper table manners he steadies the hefty pitcher with both hands while draining its contents. The disapproving expression on his partner's face and the anticipative air in his pose indicate his dismay, since the high-handled wine cup, a kantharos, he extends toward the pitcher may well be dry. The third leg panel displays not komasts, but athletes. In this scene a vigorous boxing match is in progress between a paunchy, bearded male figure on the left and a somewhat slimmer youth, or beardless athlete, on the right. Immediately behind the boxers stands a tripod, the contested prize and no doubt an inspiration to the contenders' enthusiasm. The tripod recalls the vessel on which it is actually painted; however, the example depicted in the scene has tall, slender legs, large ring handles, and is meant to be constructed of bronze.

The six creatures on the tubular body of the vase are likewise depicted in pairs and in heraldic fashion. Two frontal-faced panthers crane their necks over a palmette. Two sirens are separated by a lotus bud on a tall stem, while a pair of does inspect one another or graze placidly together. Each pair of creatures is oblivious to the others and, likewise, follows the isolated pattern established by the human figures on the separate leg panels. In contrast to the animated humans the six creatures appear lifeless, serving merely as decorative objects, and provide us with a clear indication as to where the painter's interests lie.

The Schimmel vase belongs to a series of vessels (many of them tripod-kothons) known as the Boeotian Dancers Group. Choice of figural subjects, especially the frolicking komasts, field ornaments, vase shape and most importantly the painted style indicate a common workshop for vases in the Group. Prevailing evidence suggests that the workshop was located in or near Tanagra in southeast Boeotia. This site was along a main road from Athens, and it was under Athenian influence, by way of the Attic Komast Group, that the workshop of the Boeotian Dancers Group created much of its art. The parading animals, field ornaments, and even the komasts themselves on these vases all derive from Corinthian workshops; however, these elements entered the Boeotian repertoire via Attic vases and/or vase-painters.

The shape of the tripod-kothon is designed for maximum stability. Its relatively small size indicates that it contained scented oils, a substance too precious to be lost by tipping over a vase. A lid, now lost, would have curtailed evaporation. The central spike under the bowl and the struts attached to the back of the legs are ceramic but reflect the construction of metal prototypes.

KARL KILINSKI II

Bibliography: O. W. Muscarella (ed.), *Ancient Art: The Norbert Schimmel Collection* (Mainz 1974) no 53. On the Boeotian Dancers Group: K. Kilinski, *American Journal of Archaeology* 82 (1978) 173-191. On komasts: A. Greifenhagen, *Eine attische schwarzfigurige Vasengattung und die Darstellung des Komos im VI Jahrhundert* (Königsberg 1929); A. Seeberg, *Corinthian Komos Vases* (London 1971). On homosexuality in Greece: K. J. Dover, *Greek Homosexuality* (London 1978).

56

Attic Black-Figure Kalpis

Collection of Mr. and Mrs. Edward L. Diefenthal, Metairie, Louisiana
Unattributed
Ca. 500-490 B.C.
      Height: 32.7 cm.

Quadriga

A four-horse chariot stands ready to depart, as one of the horses looks down and impatiently paws the ground. A dog stands before the horses, facing them but looking around at his tail. The tail is swung in a high arc, and a little glaze has accidentally dripped from it. In the car of the chariot stands a tall bearded driver wearing a long white *chiton*, holding the reins, and carrying in his right hand a goad (*kentron*). Since no warrior is present, perhaps the chariot is bound not for the battlefield, but rather for a competition at the games or a festival.

The kalpis is a variety of hydria in which the neck, shoulder, and body form a continuous curve. It is primarily a red-figure shape and was first introduced about 520, but there are many examples in later black-figure. The figured scene may be confined to a panel on the shoulder, as here, or extend over the bulge and onto the body, as often in red-figure. On the Diefenthal kalpis, the picture is framed below by two bands of ivy leaves without berries and on the other three sides by a double net pattern. The standing quadriga is not an uncommon subject; according to Dietrich von Bothmer, the closest parallel is on a vase in Hamburg (1908.253; *CVA* pl. 27).

Bibliography: Unpublished.

Detail of Shoulder

57

Attic Red-Figure Cup

Collection of the Virginia Museum of Fine Arts, Richmond (63.11)
Attributed to the Antiphon Painter
490-480 B.C.

Height: 9.4 cm.
Diameter (without handles): 23 cm.

Interior: Young athlete with strigil
Sides A and B: Athletes

All three scenes show young athletes in the palestra. In the tondo, a nude youth stands frontally, looking to his right. He holds a strigil, the curved metal instrument used by athletes to scrape dust, sweat, and oil off their bodies. The boy is scraping off his right wrist. In the background hangs a sponge, used by athletes in bathing.

On side A, two more youths scrape themselves with strigils. A third figure has the conventional attribute and dress of the *paidotribes*, or trainer: a voluminous cloak draped over one shoulder and a knotty stick. Usually, however, the *paidotribes* is a mature bearded man, the proprietor of the palestra (cf. [60]); this trainer is a beardless boy who appears no older than the athletes.

On side B, four nude youths stand or turn in a variety of poses. One holds a large diskos in his left hand and strides to the left, as if about to release it. One holds a strigil, apparently trying to scrape his back, while another comes up, perhaps to lend a hand. The fourth stands off to the left by himself.

Athletic subjects gave Late Archaic red-figure vase-painters an opportunity to experiment in rendering the nude male body in many different poses. Here we have a range of poses, from frontal to several varieties of three-quarter view, to a slightly awkward back view.

The Antiphon Painter was a specialist in cups, and one of his favorite subjects was athletes. His figures are usually quite lively, though not as finely drawn as those of his contemporaries, Onesimos and the Panaitian Group. He reached his mature style at the very end of the Archaic period, in the 480's.

Bibliography: Beazley, *ARV*² 1646, 13 *bis*; *Paralipomena* 521; *Ancient Art in the Virginia Museum* (Richmond 1973) 105.

Side A

Interior

Side B

147

58

Attic Black-Figure Oinochoe (White-Ground)

Collection of the Duke University Museum of Art, Durham (1969.4)
Workshop of the Athena Painter [A. Clark]
Ca. 500 B.C.
  Height: 22 cm.
  Diameter: 17 cm.

Athlete and trainer

The scene is set in the palestra, despite the vines in the background, which are only a filling ornament typical of this period, rather than an indication of locale. In the center, a well developed young athlete prepares to practice a jump. He holds a pair of bronze jumping weights (*halteres*). Facing him stands a young man in a tightly wrapped *himation*, who is probably the trainer who coaches the young jumper. At the left stands a young boy, considerably smaller than the other two. He holds a variety of accoutrements regularly used in the palestra: a strigil, or scraper, a round oil bottle, and a large spotted (hide?) bag for holding equipment. These are all tied to the knotty staff which the boy holds in his right hand. The staff should belong to the trainer and the other equipment to the jumper. Perhaps the boy is a young slave who looks after the paraphernalia of athletes and trainers.

The Duke vase is one of many late black-figure oinochoai produced by the Athena Painter's workshop. A number of these, though by no means all, were decorated in the white-ground technique (compare [17]). Among the oinochoai of this workshop Beazley distinguished several classes according to variations in shape. The Duke example, with its short neck and no collar, spreading mouth, round handle, and the figured scene occupying the whole surface, rather than framed in a panel, belongs to the Sèvres Class.

Bibliography: *Hesperia Art Bulletin* 45/46 (January, 1969) no. A 17; J. R. Mertens, *Attic White Ground* (New York 1977) 73, no. 68. Sèvres Class: Beazley, *ABV* 524-25.

59

Attic Red-Figure Cup

Collection of the Ackland Art Museum, University of North Carolina, Chapel Hill,
    Ackland Fund (66.27.4)
Workshop of the Codrus Painter
Ca. 430 B.C.
    Height: 10 cm.
    Diameter: 28.3 cm.

Interior: Archer
Sides A and B: Athletes

This cup illustrates life in the Greek palestra, a favorite theme throughout Attic red-figure vase-painting. Like many cups by the Codrus Painter and his followers, this one depicts various forms of athletic training. All the participants are male, short-haired, well built and nude. In the center of **side A** are two confronted wrestlers: one, bent over at the waist, is helpless, while the other grips him in a body hold in preparation for giving him "the heave." The contestants are flanked by a pair of bystanders who gesture toward the wrestlers as if giving advice. **On side B** a jumper takes center stage. With both arms and left leg extended, he is shown in the take-off position for the running broad jump. He is likewise framed by two fellow athletes; the one at the left with a stick is perhaps a trainer.

The subject of the tondo, an archer testing his bow, is an unusual one. Archers normally appear in military scenes where they are characterized by their non-Greek garb as foreigners, usually Scythians. This nude athlete, on the other hand, is clearly Greek, and the setting is the palestra, as indicated by the pillar or goal post at the left. This cup then documents the practice of archery as part of the athletic training of Athenian youths. While before the Persian Wars the bow had little status among the Greeks, its worth was proven at the Battle of Salamis, and by 450 B.C., the Athenian military had a trained corps of archers, who were used effectively during the Peloponnesian War. Thus, this cup, which dates to the time of the latter war, illustrates not only the athletic training of Athenian youth but their military preparation for the great conflict with Sparta.

If not by the Codrus Painter himself, this cup can be assigned to his workshop, one which favored athletic scenes. The heavy physique of the athletes, the proclivity for faces in three-quarter view, and the palmette complexes under the handles are all characteristic of this artist.

JENIFER NEILS

Bibliography: On Greek athletics: E. N. Gardiner, *Athletics of the Ancient World* (Oxford, 1930); H. A. Harris, *Sport in Greece and Rome* (London, 1972). On archery: A. M. Snodgrass, *Arms and Armour of the Greeks* (London, 1967) esp. 98-99. A late archaic cup in Boston (10.207) by Onesimos shows Greek archers in the tondo and athletes on the exterior; for a discussion of the archers: L. D. Caskey and J. D. Beazley, *Attic Vase Paintings in the Museum of Fine Arts, Boston*, Part II (Oxford, 1954) 27-28. On the Codrus Painter: Beazley, *ARV²* 1268-1275.

Side A

Interior

Side B

151

60

Attic Red-Figure Oinochoe

Collection of the New Orleans Museum of Art, Gift of Alvin P. Howard (16.11)
Manner of the Nikias Painter
Ca. 400 B.C.
     Height: 18 cm.
     Diameter: 14 cm.

Athletes and trainer

Two young nude athletes practise jumping under the watchful eye of a *paidotribes*, or trainer. The boy in the center, in mid-jump, holds the bronze jumping weights (*halteres*) used to give added momentum. Behind him a youth waits his turn, resting one hand on his hip and with the other gesturing toward the jumper. On the ground beside the jumper is a low stone slab on a flat base, perhaps a distance marker for measuring the jump.

The bearded *paidotribes* holds a long staff, hooked at the top. His ornate *himation*, a mass of delicately swirling folds, and especially the wreath he wears suggest he is not an ordinary trainer in a palestra.

Rather, he could be an official or judge at a festival or athletic games.

In the field are two round objects, one behind the trainer, the other between the two athletes, each with a dotted circle within a reserved blob. They might be diskoi, hung on the wall, or aryballoi, small round oil bottles, suspended so that we see the mouth facing out.

The vase can be dated the the very end of the fifth century and is closely related in style to the Nikias Painter, who worked mostly on larger shapes, kraters and hydrias.

Bibliography: Unpublished. Nikias Painter: Beazley, *ARV*² 1333-35.

61

Attic Red-Figure Pelike

Collection of the New Orleans Museum of Art, Gift of Alvin P. Howard (16.15)
Attributed to the Painter of London E395
Ca. 430-420 B.C.

Height: 11.9 cm.
Diameter: 11 cm.

Side A: Athlete with jumping weights and youth
Side B: Woman

On side A, a nude youth with curly hair holds a pair of *halteres*, or metal jumping weights. He strides to the right, as if preparing to make a practice jump. A second youth, clad in a long thin mantle, extends his right hand toward the first. Perhaps he is a trainer giving advice to a novice on the use of the *halteres*.

On side B, a woman stands closely wrapped in a *himation*. She is stylish, with her hair bound by a fillet and a long loop earring. She has no apparent connection with the athletes on the other side, but is a standard figure on the reverses of smaller vases of this period.

The vase was attributed by Beazley to a minor follower of the Washing Painter, who decorated many small and usually undistinguished pelikai in the years around 425 [6]. He takes his name from his fondness for scenes of women bathing.

Bibliography: Beazley, *ARV*² 1140, 3.

Side A

Side B

155

Revelry, Love and Marriage

The quintessentially Greek form of private entertainment was the symposium, an all-male drinking party. The institution was immortalized by Plato's dialogue titled *Symposium*, and in art its essence was best captured by the painters of Archaic red-figure, a century before Plato's time. The only beverage served was wine, diluted with water as much as four or five parts to one, so that enormous quantities could be consumed before (around dawn, as in Plato's version) everyone was completely inebriated. Doubtless one reason symposium scenes are so common on Attic vases is that many of these vessels were designed specifically for use on such occasions: kraters for mixing the wine with water [11, 30], psykters for cooling it, kyathoi for ladling it [49], and cups [67], kantharoi, and skyphoi [15] for drinking it.

The wine was mixed and served by nude slave boys. Although the guests were all men, there might be women present: *hetairai* (literally "companions"), professionals, often foreigners, hired for the evening. They may recline alongside the gentlemen on couches strewn with coverlets and pillows, but they are always dressed and well behaved. There was musical entertainment, somtimes a lyre played by an older man [32], but more often provided by a flute-girl. There could be singing, occasionally a dancer, and *hetairai* are often shown with *krotala*, metal castanets [66]. As the wine began to take effect, some of the company, both men and women, might play *kottabos*, hooking one finger around the handle of an empty cup and flinging the dregs at a target on the floor [32].

Hetairai were virtually the only females a freeborn unmarried young man in Athens was likely to come in contact with, owing to the general seclusion of respectable women. If his funds allowed, he could enjoy the company of a *hetaira* often [63], and scenes of sexual activity (usually not in the context of the symposium) are plentiful in red-figure. These are not married couples, but a man and a *hetaira*.

But if our young man sought a romantic friendship with a person of equal social status, in which he could be appreciated for himself and not his money, this was possible only with another male. This in part explains the prevalence of the homoerotic relationship between men and adolescent boys among the Athenian upper classes in the Archaic and Classical periods. Vases depicting the "courtship" of men and boys are much more popular in black-figure than in red [62, 64] and cease entirely by 475, but Plato's writings attest that the institution was still alive and well a century later. The longevity of this phenomenon and the apparent lack of censure must be due mainly to its confinement to a relatively small circle of Athenians, the leisured aristocracy; the upper class has never been subject to the same moral and societal restraints as everyone else.

When it came time for a man to marry, generally in his mid- or late twenties, it was usually not to a woman of his choice (or vice-versa), and the marriage may have been contracted by the families years before, when both were children. The bride was often much younger, sometimes barely adolescent. The dowry, as in some Greek villages today, was a crucial element in the whole transaction. The couple scarcely knew each other and may well never have laid eyes on each other. Nevertheless the marriage was considered of tremendous importance in binding together two families, or linking two branches of the same extended clan, and the wedding ritual and attendant celebration were a gala event occupying not just one day, like ours, but several. Preparations for a wedding, such as the ritual bathing of bride and groom or the decking out of the bride, are represented on red-figure vases, sometimes clarifying the confused testimony of the ancient sources. Perhaps the most significant event was a procession in which the bride was conducted to her new home following a banquet, signifying her transition from the family of her father to that of her husband. Occasionally we glimpse this gathering in vase-paintings [62], but its importance may also be inferred from the popularity of mythological wedding scenes, usually featuring the newly married couple in a chariot. They may be Peleus and Thetis, the parents of Achilles, Admetos and Alkestis, or Herakles and Hebe. Often a group of gods accompanies the chariot on foot, Apollo playing his lyre and all sharing a joyous exuberance that must have permeated Athenian weddings as it does weddings everywhere.

62

Attic (?) Black-Figure Tripod Pyxis

Collection of The University Museums, University of Mississippi, Phase I Cultural Center (77.3.72)
Unattributed
550-540 B.C.
>   Height: 5.5 cm.
>   Diameter: 8.5 cm.

Side A: Bride (?) and men conversing
Side B: Men and women conversing
Side C: Courtship of men and boys

The significance, if any, of the groups on **sides A and B** is uncertain. Only the gesture of the woman holding her veil before her face hints that she may be a bride; the painter probably intended no more than to provide an atmosphere of fashionable gaiety surrounding the principal scene on **side C**. This shows three stages of courtship between men and adolescent boys. Two couples are making love; in each pair the older lover (*erastes*) stands with his knees bent, clasping his beloved (*eromenos*) around the waist and resting his head on the boy's shoulder. The third couple is at an earlier stage of courtship; the man reaches toward the boy's chin with one hand and toward his genitals with the other, while the boy tries with both hands to fend him off (compare [64]). At the far right a man approaches holding a gamecock, a standard gift from a wooer to the boy he was courting. Perhaps this one is intended for the unattached youth who seems to be dancing at the far left.

This is an early example of a theme that appeared often in vase painting between about 560 and 470 B.C. Though later painters might treat such themes with more psychological subtlety, scenes of actual lovemaking are presented seriously, never becoming much more undignified or explicit than this. Scenes of heterosexual lovemaking, on the other hand, may be far more explicit, often with heavy emphasis on the grotesque and comic aspects of sex. The reason for this difference lies in Athenian social customs. Women played no part in Athenian public life. Women of good family seldom went out in public and had few opportunities to meet men socially who were not their own relatives. Marriage was a practical arrangement, undertaken to perpetuate the family and its property, and the couple might never have met before the wedding. The women who appear in scenes of drinking and lovemaking are not wives but hired entertainers and prostitutes, many of them slaves, with whom a serious love relationship would be impossible. For an Athenian man of the upper classes, the only real chance for an emotionally satisfying love affair with a social equal was with a boy or youth of his own class. In Athens and most other Greek cities such relationships were not only permitted but approved and praised as the source of one of life's greatest joys. For the boy, such a relationship was considered beneficial and educational, giving him a recognized place in the male society in which he would spend most of his adult life.

LUCY TURNBULL

Bibliography: D. M. Robinson, "Unpublished Greek Vases in the Robinson Collection," *American Journal of Archaeology* 60 (1956), 1-25, pl. 1, 5-7. For courtship scenes in general: J. D. Beazley, "Some Attic Vases in the Cyprus Museum," *Proceedings of the British Academy* 33 (1947), 3-31. For the place of such relationships in Athenian society: H. A. Shapiro, "Courtship Scenes in Attic Vase Painting," *American Journal of Archaeology* 85 (1981), 133-143.

Side A

Side B

Side C

159

63

Attic Red-Figure Oinochoe

Collection of Gilbert M. Denman, Jr., San Antonio
Attributed to the Berlin Painter
Ca. 490-480 B.C.
  Height: 29.2 cm.
  Diameter: 12.7 cm.

Youth and seated woman

This elegant oinochoe, with its trefoil lip and high-swung handle terminating in a painted palmette, illustrates a tryst between a young man and a woman. The locale is clearly the *gynaikeion* or women's quarters; the woman is seated as if at home, and a mirror is hanging on the wall above her head. Her seat is a *klismos* or high-backed chair equipped with a dotted cushion. Her appearance is rather prim and matronly, despite her prominent breasts. She is garbed in a *chiton* and *himation*, and her curly hair is tied up in a fillet. Her finery includes a pendant necklace and at least one spiral bracelet in added red. Leaning towards her on his staff is a mantle-clad youth wearing a wreath in his short hair. He is a visitor and his mission is made explicit by the object clutched in his left hand, a coin purse. While some scholars have taken such scenes to represent a husband bringing home his pay, others interpret it not as a conjugal encounter but as a commercial venture, that is, a man negotiating for the favors of a *hetaira* (courtesan). That the latter interpretation is correct is here verified by the sexual implications of the other attributes. The youth is handing the woman a flower, while she appears to be tickling him with a long tendril. The fact that the picture appears on a wine jug used by men at their drinking parties perhaps also supports this view.

This vase is considered by Beazley to be an early work of the Berlin Painter, one of the most prolific late archaic pot-painters in the Athenian Kerameikos. While he generally preferred amorous pursuits, this scene of quiet dalliance is admirably suited to the shape of the oinochoe.

JENIFER NEILS

Bibliography: Beazley, *Paralipomena* 345, 184 *ter*. On scenes of youths and *hetairai*: G. Rodenwaldt, "Spinnende Hetären," *Archäologischer Anzeiger* 1932, 7-21.

See color frontspiece

64

Attic Black-Figure Eye Cup

Collection of the Cummer Gallery of Art, Jacksonville (AP.66.28)
Group of Courting Cups [Shapiro]
Ca. 520-500 B.C.
  Height: 10 cm.
  Diameter: 21.25 cm.

Side A: Man courting a boy
Side B: Youth riding a hippalektryon

Scenes of homosexual courting between men and boys first appear on Attic black-figure vases soon before the middle of the sixth century. In the third and especially the last quarter of the century this becomes one of the often repeated genre scenes in vase-painting. After 500 the scene's popularity falls off sharply, and after about 475 it disappears entirely. Well over 100 representations are known in all.

Sir John Beazley distinguished three stages in the courtship, and all painted scenes illustrate one of the three: an initial encounter (type alpha); the giving of gifts by the older man to the youth (type beta); and the consummation, in which the pair are intertwined (type gamma; cf. [62]). Type alpha is depicted most often, and the Jacksonville vase is a typical example.

On side A, the older lover (*erastes*) stands at the left and reaches out both hands to his beloved (*eromenos*). With his left hand he chucks the boy's chin, as if to distract him while the lowered right hand moves in on its target. The boy reaches out with his left, perhaps a gesture of diffidence. Both are entirely nude, as is the rule in black-figure; in red-figure versions one or both will often be at least partly draped. The boy's hair is long and flows freely in the back, while the man's is bound by a fillet. The wooer's knees are usually bent to compensate for his greater stature.

On side B, a youth rides a hippalektryon, a mythical creature, half horse and half cock. It is one of many hybrids - fantastic beasts composed of elements of two or more animals or, like the centaur and the siren, part animal, part human - who populate Archaic Greek

vase-painting and sculpture. Most hybrids seem to have come into Greece from the East, but there is no prototype of the hippalektryon in Egyptian or Near Eastern Art. Nevertheless it appears regularly on Attic vases (and only Attic) from the second quarter of the sixth century down to the end of the century or a little later. The rider is usually, as here, an unarmed youth. The hippalektryon has no mythology and is in fact scarcely mentioned by Greek writers: once in a lost play of Aeschylus, as a device painted on a ship, and once by Aristophanes, who implies that by his time (late fifth century) the average Athenian had never heard of it. But the vase-painters are consistent in portraying it with the hind legs of a cock and the forelegs of a horse, though attached to a cock's breast.

This cup may be assigned to a group of nearly thirty vases assembled by Beazley in *Paralipomena* as the Group of Courting Cups. They are eye cups (see [13]) of Type A (a shallow bowl, plain lip, short, splaying foot with a moulding separating it from the bowl). The whites of the eyes are filled in with white paint, unlike those of earlier eye cups, which are mostly left in outline. All but a few of the Courting Cups have a man and boy on one side, and many repeat the motif on both sides. One has a youth on a hippalektryon on both sides (*Paralipomena* 83,22). The choice of the courtship to decorate drinking cups that would be used at all-male symposia is not surprising; the monotonous repetition of the same formula and the hasty draughtsmanship show that the motif is nearing the end of its artistic life.

Bibliography: Unpublished. On courtship scenes: J. D. Beazley, *Some Attic Vases in the Cyprus Museum* (London 1948) 6-31; H. A. Shapiro, "Courtship Scenes in Attic Vase-Painting," *American Journal of Archaeology* 85 (1981) 133-43. On the hippalektryon: D. von Bothmer, in *Bulletin of the Metropolitan Museum of Art* 11 (1953) 132-36. Group of Courting Cups: Beazley, *Paralipomena* 82-83.

Side A

Side B

163

65

Attic Red-Figure Lekythos

Collection of the University of Arkansas Museum, Fayetteville (57-27-42)
Attributed to the Painter of London E342
Ca. 460 B.C.
Height: 29.6 cm.
Diameter: 9.9 cm.

Youth and Girl

A youth stands in profile to the right, stretching out both hands to a young woman, who stands frontally but looks sideways at him. He is dressed in a *himation*; she wears a *peplos* and a thin wrap, one end of it hanging from her left arm, the other end held in her right hand. In her other hand she holds a tall upright staff. The boy offers her an object, sizeable and slightly oblong: perhaps a pomegranate, or else another fruit or a ball of wool. Two strokes in added red projecting from the top could represent the stem of a fruit.

Pomegranates were always a symbol of fertility in Greece, owing to the profusion of juicy seeds. Several myths allude to the erotic associations of the fruit, most notably the story of Persephone, who was raped by the god Hades, then was obliged to remain half the year with her new husband in the Underworld after she had eaten of a pomegranate. Hence the pomegranate appears occasionally in vase-paintings as a love gift from a young man to his intended, or from husband to wife, as on a pyxis in Athens (Beazley, *Paralipomena* 391, 88 *bis*). Various other fruits and balls of wool serve the same purpose on red-figure vases, as romantic love tokens between the sexes. For the object on the Fayetteville lekythos, R. F. Sutton compares that on a contemporary lekythos in Cassel (Beazley, *Paralipomena* 402, Nikon Painter, 33 *bis*).

The staff which the woman holds, normally an attribute only of goddesses and queens, suggests that the painter may have intended to create a heroized version of a popular romantic genre scene.

The vase was assigned by Beazley to an artist of the Early Classical period who painted many small neck-amphoras, but also lekythoi and other small vase shapes. Many of his scenes show a young man and woman, sometimes together but more often on either side of the same vase. In four instances, other types of gifts are exchanged (Beazley, *ARV*² 668, 29-31 and 33).

Bibliography: Beazley, *ARV*² 669, 45; Q. Maule, in *American Journal of Archaeology* 75 (1971) 87-88 and pl. 21, 6. On love gifts of fruit and wool: R. F. Sutton, *The Interaction Between Men and Women Portrayed on Attic Red-figure Pottery* (Diss. University of North Carolina, Chapel Hill 1981) 320-26.

165

66

Attic Red-Figure Kylix

Collection of the University of Arkansas Museum, Fayetteville (56.25.15)
Attributed to Oltos [Hecht]
Ca. 510 B.C.

> Height: 6.7 cm.
> Diameter: 18.6 cm.
> Diameter with handles: 24.5 cm.

Interior: Woman with *krotala*

This simple cup, undecorated on the exterior, has a single figure within a reserved circle on the interior. She is a buxom woman, dressed in a long pleated *chiton* with an ample overfold at the waist. Her curly, black hair is tied with a long red fillet and she sports a round, black earring. She is moving to the left, perhaps dancing, as she holds a pair of *krotala* or castanets in her hands.

The woman with her pinched nose, frowning mouth and excessively long feet is typically Oltan. Oltos, whose name is known from two signed cups, was a prolific cup-painter in the early years of red-figure (ca. 525-500 B.C.). He depicted many such music-making women whose identification is determined by their context. When accompanied by satyrs, they are clearly maenads; when nude or at a symposium, obviously *hetairai* or prostitutes. Since neither this singleton nor her "sister" on a similar cup at Mount Holyoke College (Beazley, *Paralipomena* 328, 127 *ter*) has a clear-cut context, they remain simply dancing women.

JENIFER NEILS

Bibliography: *Vente Publique X* 22-23 June 1951 (Bâle: Monnaies et Médailles) pl. 20, no. 413; Beazley, *ARV²* 66, 130; Q. Maule, "Greek Vases in Arkansas," *American Journal of Archaeology* 75 (1971) 86-87, pl. 21, figs. 1-2.
On Oltos: A. Bruhn, *Oltos and Early Red-Figure Vase Painting* (Copenhagen, 1943).

67

Attic Red-Figure Cup

Collection of the John and Mable Ringling Museum of Art, Sarasota (1600. G3)
Unattributed
500-475 B. C.
        Height: 12.7 cm.
        Diameter (with handles): 36.56 cm.

Interior: Youth reclining at a symposium

The exterior of the cup is undecorated. In the tondo, a beardless youth reclines on a *kline*, or couch, and leans against a thick cushion with striped cover. His legs are enveloped in a heavy cloak, one end of which is draped over his left arm, leaving his chest bare. He also wears a fillet in his short, cap-like hair, decorated with leaves. In each outstretched hand the youth holds a skyphos, a type of drinking vessel (cf. [15]) with a considerably larger capacity than a typical cup such as this one. In the background hangs an object of spotted animal hide, probably a flute case.

The scene is clearly meant to be understood as an excerpt from a gathering of several drinkers. The youth sits up and twists his head, as if to look back at a companion on the next *kline*, and one of the two skyphoi must be intended for a fellow symposiast. The flute case alludes to the musical entertainment popular at such parties.

Along the upper border of the scene is the inscription HO ΠΑΙΣ , completed by the word KAVOΣ in the exergue beneath the *kline*: *Ho pais kalos* ("the boy is beautiful"). This is typical of the many inscriptions on Attic vases praising the beauty of a boy, often naming him (cf. [19]), but just as often limited to the simple formula as we have it here. The formula may even be added to scenes in which, unlike this one, there is no one to whom it may plausibly refer.

Bibliography: Unpublished. On kalos inscriptions: D. M. Robinson and E. J. Fluck, *A Study of the Greek Love-Names* (Baltimore 1937).

Bell Krater

Column Krater

Kyathos

Lekythos

Oinochoe

Skyphos

Hydria
(Kalpis)

Squat
Lekythos

Rhyton

Pelike

Plate

Belly Amphora

Cup
(Kylix)

Aryballos

Alabastron

Tripod-Pyxis
(Kothon)

Panathenaic
Amphora

Neck Amphora

Glossary of Shapes in the Exhibition

Alabastron: a flask with an elongated body, rounded bottom, and narrow neck, used to contain perfume. Egyptian vessels made of alabaster were the models for the Attic vase.
[7, 33]

Amphora: a two-handled jar used for storing oil, wine, and grain.

The *Belly Amphora*, also called a one-piece Amphora or Panel Amphora, has a continuous curve from neck to body.
[22, 25, 27]

The *Neck Amphora* has the neck set off from the body by a change in contour.
[2, 8, 10, 12, 14, 16, 23, 24, 29, 31, 35, 37, 48]

The *Panathenaic Amphora* has a broad body which tapers sharply downwards.
[1, 40]

Aryballos: a small bottle with a globular body and narrow neck, used by athletes to contain oil.
[46]

Cup: (sometimes called a *Kylix*): a drinking vessel which has a shallow bowl, two handles, and a tall foot.
[13, 19, 21, 28, 53, 57, 59, 64, 66, 67]

Hydria: a water jar with a broad belly and narrow neck. It has two horizontal handles for lifting, and a third, vertical handle for pouring.

The *Kalpis* is distinguished by having a continuous curve from lip to foot.
[38, 51, 56]

Krater: a large vessel with a wide mouth and broad body used for mixing wine and water.

The *Bell Krater* has horizontal, lug handles and a bell-shaped body.
[30]

The *Column Krater* has vertical, columnar handles.
[4, 11, 39]

Kyathos: a dipper with a single, high-swung handle used for ladling wine.
[49]

Lekythos: a slender jug with a narrow neck and one handle, used to contain oil.
[5, 9, 18, 26, 41, 42, 43, 44, 45, 52, 65]

The *Squat Lekythos* has a broad body and a curving shoulder.
[50]

Oinochoe: a small pitcher used for pouring wine, which often has a trefoil mouth.
[17, 20, 47, 58, 60, 63]

Pelike: a variety of amphora with a lower center of gravity, and a continuous curve from neck to body.
[6, 34, 36, 61]

Plate: a round plaque made for dedicatory purposes, often with suspension holes.
[3]

Rhyton: a handled drinking cup attached to a molded animal head, sometimes on a footed base.
[32]

Skyphos: a deep drinking cup with nearly vertical sides, and two horizontal handles.
[15]

Tripod-Pyxis (Kothon): a type of lidded box with three broad legs in place of a cylindrical body, used to contain cosmetics.
[55, 62]

Photographic Credits

Ackland Art Museum, University of North Carolina   59

University of Arkansas Museum   34, 65, 66

Colonial Williamsburg   32 (rollout)

Edward L. Diefenthal   13, 15, 18, 21, 22, 27, 41, 45, 53, 56, 60, 61

Foto D. Widmer, Basel   11

The Museum of Fine Arts, Houston   3, 51

North Carolina Museum of Art   35, 47

John and Mable Ringling Museum of Art   8, 17, 48, 67

Museum of Fine Arts, St. Petersburg, Florida   2

San Antonio Museum Association   25

Bill J. Strehorn, Dallas   28, 55

Trahan-Brocato Photo, New Orleans   14, 42, 43, 44

The University Museums, University of Mississippi   5, 6, 7, 16, 19, 23, 31, 36, 54, 62

Virginia Museum of Fine Arts, Richmond   24, 32, 33, 37, 38, 57

175